DATE DUE

Reflecting
the
Character
of
Christ

Reflecting
the
Character
of
Christ

DR. LES CARTER

A
JANET
THOMA
BOOK

THOMAS NELSON PUBLISHERS
Nashville • Atlanta • London • Vancouver

Published in Nashville, Tennessee, by Thomas Nelson, Inc., Publishers, and distributed in Canada by Word Communications, Ltd., Richmond, British Columbia.

The Bible version used in this publication is THE NEW KING JAMES VERSION. Copyright © 1979, 1980, 1982, 1990 Thomas Nelson, Inc., Publishers.

Anecdotes and clients' stories in this volume are composites of actual cases or hypothetical situations based on the author's experiences. Facts and details have been changed to protect the identities of those involved.

Library of Congress Cataloging-in-Publication Data

Carter, Les.
    Reflecting the character of Christ : his kindness, his confidence, his grace / Les Carter.
        p.   cm.
    Includes bibliographical references.
    ISBN 0-7852-8063-4
    1. Jesus Christ—Psychology. 2. Christian life. 3. Personality—Religious aspects—Christianity. I. Title.
BT590.P9C37 1995
232.9'03—dc20
                                          94-37284
                                            CIP

Printed in the United States of America.

1 2 3 4 5 6 — 00 99 98 97 96 95

*To my parents, Ed and Anne Carter,
for they have been lifelong illustrations
of the character of Christ.*

Contents

Acknowledgments

A special thank you is due to Irene Swindell for her valuable role in preparing the manuscript. Also, the editorial staff of Thomas Nelson Publishers, especially Janet Thoma, deserve major credit for the way they helped put my thoughts into words.

As Janet and I reviewed sections of the book, she repeatedly asked where my ideas came from. My understanding of Christ's mission and personality was shaped very early in life due to the influence and hands-on teaching of my parents, Ed and Anne Carter.

His Presence:

Practicing the Character of Christ

Suppose you could somehow suspend time and spend a day talking with any historical figure. Who would you select to spend that day with?

It's fun dreaming of the possibilities, isn't it? You might have a favorite relative you would like to see again, perhaps a deceased parent or grandparent. Or you might choose a prominent political figure—Abraham Lincoln or Benjamin Franklin—or one of the giants of the Christian faith—Luther or Calvin or Augustine.

There are many such persons I'd like to spend a day with; but if pressed to name only *one*, I'd have no trouble making my decision. I would choose Jesus.

Just to see His face and hear His voice!

I would take Jesus back to a place that was one of my favorite hangouts as a boy, a shaded creekbank near my childhood home in Georgia where the woods were so thick you could barely see the houses just a hundred yards away. The trees formed a perfect canopy over the creek, blocking the scorching summer sun and providing a cool, fresh fragrance and natural air-conditioning for boys looking to lose themselves in hours of play and adventure. Yes, that's where I would take Jesus. We would kick back on the cool ground and talk.

There would be so many questions to ask: "Jesus, we know so little about Your boyhood years in Nazareth. What was childhood like for You? What did You do for fun? How did You play with the other kids? As a child, did You know God's purpose for Your life?"

I'd want to get the inside scoop on His disciples. "How did they budget their time between their ministry and their families? What was Peter like? Were You really related to John and James, as some have speculated? What about Matthew? Being a tax collector, was he unpopular with the rest of the fellows?" No telling what sorts of stories Jesus could share!

And to hear Him recount some of the miracles—what a thought! "Jesus, when You turned the fishes and loaves into a meal for thousands, what went through Your mind? What did You say about it to the disciples the next day?

Whatever happened to the paralytic man who was lowered through the roof? And the raising of Lazarus from the dead . . . it was such an emotional experience for You. What were You feeling as You stood outside the tomb?"

But knowing Jesus, I suspect He wouldn't let this imaginary day go by without turning the spotlight back onto me: "Les, what about your life? What would you consider your successes and failures to be? Tell Me about your work as a counselor. And Les, what personal matters do you struggle with most? What hopes do you cling to? And what about your life at home with your wife and kids? What's a typical day like? Do you understand God's purpose for *your* life?"

Throughout the day, we would talk freely about personal circumstances, about religious life, philosophies, and social responsibilities. We would have no shortage of subjects to discuss, though we *would* have a shortage of time to discuss them. The day would fly by too quickly.

Now let's stay with this imaginary scene just awhile longer. Suppose my day with Jesus has ended. A week passes by, then a month, a year, five years, ten years. Now I'm looking back on that day I spent with Him. What impressions would dominate my mind?

Unquestionably, I would have a keener insight into Jewish history, and I would know more about some fine points of theology, doctrine, philosophies, and ideas. But I doubt those things would be foremost in my memories of that day.

More than anything, I would undoubtedly recall the *character* of Jesus. I would smile as I reflected on the gentleness of His spirit and the confidence in His voice. I would remember His passionate conviction and, at the same time, His remarkable willingness to accept differences.

I would remember feeling loved as never before.

UNDERSTANDING JESUS' CHARACTER

One day there will be no more need to imagine such things because Jesus will become fully real to me, and I'll have an eternity to know Him through and through. But until that day, I'm left to speculate on who He really is. As I do, I picture Him as a caring friend, a compassionate comforter, a wise and trusted mentor. *Who* Jesus is supersedes *what* Jesus did. Knowing His character is a prerequuisite to understanding His deeds.

Before Jesus ascended to heaven He told His followers, "You shall receive power when the Holy Spirit has come upon you; and you shall be witnesses to Me" (Acts 1:8).

Many people hear these words strictly in the performance sense, interpreting them to mean we are to represent Jesus by doing good deeds and speaking the correct words. But that does not take Jesus' directive far enough. Being a witness for Christ involves more than just what we say and do; it requires a transformation of our inner characters. We are to represent Jesus, not just by our words and deeds, but by reflecting His character . . . His kindness, His confidence, His grace. Until we reflect the characteristics of Christ Himself, we do not fully understand His command to be His witnesses.

THE CHRISTIAN'S DILEMMA

As you can imagine, I encounter a wide array of personalities in my counseling practice. Since the Minirth Meier New Life Clinic is known as a Christian clinic, many of my counselees are either church members or are related to church members. In spite of their exposure to reliable teaching, they are still prone to destructive emotions: depression, anxiety, anger, bitterness, pride. I find that most of them know the basics of Christianity, but they have not developed a close relationship with Jesus. Their emotional pain tells me they are in desperate need of a more intimate walk with the Savior.

One person who comes to mind is Tammy, a forty-year-old woman who was reared as the daughter of church-going parents and whose husband was a deacon and Sunday school teacher. She and her husband were in church every time the doors opened, yet Tammy had struggled for years with secret anger and insecurities.

"Something's not right in my life," she told me. "I know I shouldn't have the problems I do, but they persist. I live a clean life; my husband and I don't go to wild parties. We spend lots of time with our children, and they're involved in sports and church programs. But I have always had a problem with frustration. It follows me wherever I go."

"From what you are saying, I would assume your frus-

trations are brought out by the busyness of your family,"
I told her. "Some days must get pretty hectic."

"*Life* is hectic," Tammy admitted. "From the moment I
get up to the time I lie down at night, something is happening. I have to keep on top of the kids' school and sports
activities, and I'm involved in a Bible study at church, so
I'm always moving. To add to it, my parents are older now,
so I try to touch base with them two or three times a week.
I try to keep things as organized as I can, but sometimes I
feel like I'm just under the pile."

"How have you attempted to cope with your emotional
ups and downs?"

"Oh, I don't know. I mean, I try to talk about it to my
husband—he's not completely insensitive to my problems—but still, he's limited in what he can do to fix things.
My friends are just as busy as I am, so I can't go to them
constantly for a bailout. I just try to do the best I can, but
it seems I'm constantly tense and on edge."

I asked her, "Does your Christian faith help you tackle
your problems?"

"Well, yes. It's nice to know that heaven is in my future,
and I do enjoy my friendships with other Christians. But I
would be reluctant to expose too many of my problems to
these friends because I don't want to scare any of them
away."

"You believe your Christian friends like to keep things
slotted into their predictable grooves?"

"That's exactly it. It's hard to be *real*, to be myself, when
I feel like I've got to be such a good Christian all the time."

Tammy's dilemma was classic for Bible-believing

Christians. To her, Christianity was a duty that was becoming increasingly wearisome as each year went by. She was burdened by the assumption that her faith required her to constantly perform her duties in a way that would bring no disrespect upon herself and her family. As her fatigue and frustration mounted, she felt forced to tightly suppress her real emotions; as a result, her feelings increasingly built up within her, creating an underlying tension that fueled her stress and irritability.

In counseling, I work with many people like Tammy to help them understand why they respond to life as they do. Many common themes tend to surface during this counseling work, and those themes can be altered to make life more enjoyable and less tense.

After several months of counseling, Tammy told me, "It's odd to admit, but now that I realize I don't have to live with an edge of frustration, I'm being forced to think about how I want to project myself more positively to others. I'm in my forties, and you would think I would have that figured out by now!"

I smiled as she spoke, mostly because I could personally relate to her words. I suggested, "Most of us spend so much time thinking about what we should *do* that we don't put enough thought into who we want to *be*."

"Just a few months ago I wouldn't have understood that, but now I know what you mean. Too often, outer qualities seem to take priority over inner character."

"Exactly!" I said, agreeing with her completely. Then I shared my thoughts about the example set by Jesus in the way He related to those around Him.

"Tammy, let's consider what your inner character could be like if you truly incorporated your relationship with Jesus into your personality," I suggested. "If we had tried to discuss this three or four months ago, I'm afraid you would have taken my encouragement as one more duty to perform. But you seem to understand now that Christianity is not obligation-driven living. It is a relationship with Jesus that, in turn, affects how you relate with others."

She nodded slowly, "My frustration was caused by my emphasis on my performance. I'd like that to change; I'm committed to Christianity, but I want it to be a different brand of Christianity than it was before."

For instance, she came to see the value of patience in her home. This meant pushing her husband and children less insistently to keep up trivial duties and spending more time in reflective conversation, being a more active listener. Likewise, she learned the value of sometimes saying no to requests for committee work at church. She reasoned that too much religious-looking activity had actually sapped her of her desire to be spiritually drawn to God.

FINDING STRENGTH TO CHANGE

How about you? When you interact with others are you more concerned with your external traits than your internal qualities? If you were to refocus, as Tammy did, what would be the first things you would change? Your acceptance of others? Your willingness to forgive? Your confidence? Would you incorporate more kindness and warmth? Greater firmness?

All of us have inner traits we need to change. Those changes can only occur when we commit ourselves to a better understanding of Christ's character and a stronger willingness to allow the Holy Spirit to direct us in our efforts to project His presence to others.

For too many years I allowed my Christian walk to be determined by human expectations . . . and they were becoming increasingly burdensome. Being in the public eye because of my speaking, writing, and radio activities, I had become adept at determining religiously correct or acceptable behaviors, then living accordingly. Likewise, as an active member of my local church, I realized that my works had to be above reproach because I was being carefully monitored by those who take it upon themselves to determine if I was acting as a member in good standing. I've even felt as if I had to behave properly to keep the members of my extended family appeased, assuming it was necessary to stay in good stead with them.

I was looking to all the wrong sources to keep myself going as a Christian, and in the meantime I was neglecting to draw my strength from the One who is the foundation of my identity. I needed to turn my attention back to Jesus. I needed to look at His life and ask, Who is He? What is so unique about Him? Why do I worship Him? How can I pattern my life after *His* and not after human expectations?

As I have reexamined the life of Jesus, I have discovered

that He probably would not fit into many modern religious circles, just as He did not fit into those traditional religious groups two thousand years ago. I saw an intensely personable man, keenly attuned to the needs and feelings of those around Him but many times overlooking religiously incorrect behaviors.

Can you relate? Have you ever been in the place where I've been, living the socially prescribed religious life while losing sight of the Savior? If so, you, too, need to shed yourself of human burdens and let Jesus become your centerpiece once again. The result can be a rejuvenation in your walk with Him.

In this book, we will explore, one by one, some of the personality qualities that made Jesus the appealing person He was. In doing so, we will create a composite picture of the healthy personality, which can serve as a model for our lives today.

You might want to set a goal of working through one chapter a week, using the chapter and its corresponding Scripture passages as a framework for your daily devotions. The discussion questions in the back of the book will be helpful in guiding your further thinking, either as an individual or as part of a group study.

By no means will this study be exhaustive. After all, how can we possibly comprehend all there is to know about the One who is so far beyond our realm? Nonetheless, by studying His life, His example, we can be challenged to focus more effectively on the witness we can have for Him in our daily lives.

As you continue through this book, do so in prayer.

Pray that you will be challenged, not just to learn new behaviors, but that you will be used by God to show Jesus to your world. Just as you can imagine how Christ's physical presence would revolutionize your life, imagine how Christ's qualities in you could bring a renewed purpose to your relationships with those close to you.

— 2 —

His Humility:

From the Great Throne to a Lowly Manger

Revelation 5:1–14; Revelation 21; Luke 2:1–20

Each time I read Revelation 21 my mind is dazzled with its pictures of heaven's glory. We can safely assume that heaven is so incomprehensibly beautiful no human description can fully capture what we will one day experience. The beauty of the New Jerusalem is externally appealing: walls of crystal clear jasper, gates of pearl, streets of gold. And it is internally appealing as well: a home of perpetual bliss without any pain or suffering or death. The written portrait of heaven in the Bible tells us, in essence, "Be prepared for an experience that will never grow weary or become boringly familiar, for it will be like nothing you now know!"

Yet to get a real picture of heaven, I like to back up a few pages and read Revelation 5, where an angel issues the challenge for one to come forward to open God's book of seven seals, the deed to planet Earth. There is a moment of silent anguish as no one is found worthy—not the angels or the four living creatures or the twenty-four elders. No one. Then Christ, described as both the Lion and the Lamb, takes center stage.

Songs break out in heaven as He alone is capable of opening the seals. I try to picture in my mind the enormity of the throng singing to Him; then I try to imagine the ecstasy of this spontaneous outburst of worship by myriads of people. They shout the worthiness of the Lamb to receive "power and riches and wisdom, and strength and honor and glory and blessing!" (v. 12). This ultimate worship service most assuredly sets the pace for many more to come. It is obvious that, if nothing else, heaven is a place where God is fully recognized as God, deservedly shown the highest esteem.

Now shift gears and turn your focus to Luke 2, the familiar story of Jesus' birth in Bethlehem. Once again He is the center of attention, but not as King of kings. He is there as a helpless baby, ready to become a fellow participant in the human struggle. The same Jesus who is central to all of heaven has done the unthinkable. He has stepped away from God's throne to take His place among sinners—shepherds and common folk, huddled in a barn.

Can you grasp the enormity of this event in the manger? Only a face-to-face meeting with the Lamb in heaven will let us truly appreciate His incarnation. When we see Jesus robed in the glory that is rightfully His, we will be truly awed at His willingness to embrace humanity in this way, and we will understand that His greatness is anchored in the unlikely characteristic of humility.

Humility is implied throughout the story of Jesus' life on earth. Joseph, the carpenter from Nazareth, had traveled to Bethlehem with Mary, his wife-to-be, to register for the census. Mary and Joseph were certainly looked upon with derision because she was pregnant before marriage. How could they possibly explain God's part in this situation to anyone who did not know them well? Would anyone listen to *you* straight-faced if you said, "My child was conceived by the Holy Spirit"? As you imagine this scene, think about Mary and Joseph humbly determining to endure the whispers and oblique comments that came their way.

We also know that the couple came from Nazareth, a town in northern Galilee that was known for its rough-and-tumble reputation. One of Jesus' followers, Nathanael, later asked, "Can anything good come out of Nazareth?" (John 1:46). God could have selected a more suitable place for His Son's parents to reside, but He was making a point: His Son would be the embodiment of humility; He would identify with the ordinary.

When Joseph and Mary arrived in Bethlehem they

found no place to stay until an innkeeper graciously offered the use of his stable. Sometime that night Mary went into labor, and instead of benefiting from the customary assistance of her mother or a midwife, she gave birth to her son surrounded by farm animals. Nothing noble or glorious about those circumstances! If anything, you would feel pity for this teenage girl forced to give birth to a special child so far from the comforts of home. God was again making the statement: Humility, not grandiosity, would be the cornerstone of Jesus' personality, undergirding His character and guiding His every behavior.

When royalty is born, a proud proclamation is given to the subjects of the kingdom. Jesus' royal birth was no exception, though His subjects were not of noble lineage. The angels were sent as messengers of God to announce His birth to the shepherds. We can surmise that the shepherds' selection to hear the news was consistent with the theme of humility since they were considered common laborers. But why shepherds? Why not wheat farmers? Or carpenters? Or food merchants? Or blacksmiths?

I believe shepherds were given the first announcement because it was their job to see that the sheep were unharmed. Many of their sheep were undoubtedly going to be slaughtered one day at the temple as sacrificial offerings for sin, and the shepherds protected them so they were unblemished and thus worthy of being used as a sacrifice. I suspect that, although the shepherds did not know it, God saw their work as vital to His redemptive plan, so He chose these unlikely subjects to hear the first announcement of His Son's birth.

As Jesus' ministry unfolded in later years, humility continued to be central to His lifestyle. When He set aside His work as a carpenter, He did not go to the affluent suburbs or position Himself with the elite to find a constituency. Instead, He chose the downtrodden and the uneducated, who knew little more than mammoth struggles as a way of life. He even associated with beggars, lepers, and prostitutes. His theme? "Come to Me, *all* you who labor and are heavy laden, and I will give you rest" (Matt. 11:28, emphasis mine). Why did He make such a point to include needy people? Because humility was the central trait of His public life.

As Jesus sought a group of twelve to become His inner circle, did He go to the seminaries to interview the top intellects of the religious world? Not at all. He rounded up a few crusty fishermen, a tax collector, a political zealot, a doubting skeptic. These became the chosen ones who would be entrusted with the message of His mission.

During his three-year public life, Jesus had no home of His own. He owned no property and had the barest of material possessions, living on the generosity of contributors. He endured chilly, inclement weather. He certainly suffered through the same physical aches and pains you and I know; no doubt He developed calluses, got sunburned, fought off gnats and mosquitoes, and put up with the common cold.

And remember, this is the same Christ who was the center of that grand worship service in heaven, the same One who was worthy to receive "power and riches and wisdom, and strength and honor and glory and blessing."

But now the highest King lived in lowliness, and He did it for one reason: to demonstrate that God honors humility.

The apostle Paul told the early Philippians to adopt this trait: "Let this mind be in you which was also in Christ Jesus, who, being in the form of God, did not consider it robbery to be equal with God" (Phil. 2:5–6).

Paul was mindful of the hook Satan used in the Garden of Eden to lure Adam and Eve into defiance of God. "Eat of the Tree of Knowledge of Good and Evil," Satan had said seductively, "and you will be like God" (see Gen. 3). His enticement caused Adam and Eve to look inward rather than Godward for their direction in life. By commanding Adam to refrain from eating of this tree, God had communicated, *I am the only One who holds ultimate knowledge of right and wrong. Submit to My authority, and I will guide you in successful living.* In contrast, when Satan told Eve she could be like God, he was communicating, *Become focused on your own preferences of right and wrong; be your own ultimate authority. Be consumed with your own cravings.*

OVERCOMING PRIDE: THE OPPOSITE OF HUMILITY

When Adam and Eve stepped into Satan's trap, a new characteristic became part of their character: sinful pride, the preoccupation with their own desires and preferences. The opposite of humility. The craving to be in control.

At the moment pride took root, their ideal existence crumbled. Mistrust, fear, blame, insecurity, guilt, anger, and isolation came crashing in on them.

This pride has remained a central component of the personality of Adam's descendants, including you and me. It is at the base of any troublesome trait you can imagine: impatience, pouting, insecurity, arguing, punitive silence, lust, domination, excessive sensitivity, chronic tardiness, judgmental spirit, laziness, inattentiveness. You name it; if the trait is on the sin side of the ledger, it is propelled by pride.

To illustrate how natural it is to have the trait of pride, rather than humility, consider how many of the following statements you can relate to. Be honest!

- When someone else is speaking, I feel an urge to interrupt with my own thoughts on the subject.
- I appear patient on the outside, but inwardly I struggle with impatience.
- I don't easily absorb someone's feedback when he or she is talking with me about one of my problems.
- I have been so consumed with my own thoughts that I have ignored what someone was saying to me.
- Sometimes I worry about my standing with others, and this worry causes me to struggle with insecurity.

In all likelihood, we can each relate to some, if not all, of these tendencies; no one is completely immune. Here's one hint at recognizing the source of the weakness: Look back over these statements and note the frequent occurrence of *I*.

If pride is at the core of all troublesome traits, it stands to reason that humility is necessary for the truly desirable traits: kindness, forgiveness, love, contentment, patience, responsible assertiveness, listening, encouragement, joy, restraint. Each of these characteristics is possible only after we choose to set aside our preoccupation with ourselves in favor of God's desires.

Jesus entered humanity to destroy our pride and revive our humility. As the "new Adam," He would model an entirely different, God-pleasing way of life, and it would be anchored in humility.

The apostle Paul described Jesus' humility this way: "[He] made Himself of no reputation, taking the form of a bondservant, and coming in the likeness of men. And being found in appearance as a man, He humbled Himself and became obedient to the point of death, even the death of the cross" (Phil. 2:7–8). Pride was not a part of Jesus' character. He lived totally for God's glory, not His own.

I have found that I can be humble only when I begin by purposely giving up my self-centeredness.

Giving Up Self-Centeredness

In the summer of 1980, I was nearly killed in a water-skiing accident. After plowing into a cluster of tree stumps on my skis, my injuries included twelve compound fractures of my legs, my pelvis, and my right arm. There were also internal injuries and lung problems. An emergency team of paramedics, doctors, and nurses literally pulled me back from death's door, and to this day I am extremely grateful to all of them.

During my initial eight-week stay in the hospital, I met

Miguel, a recent refugee from Nicaragua who worked as an orderly there. In his early thirties, Miguel already had sprinkles of gray around his temples. A perpetual smile brightened his round face and soft, dark eyes, and his voice was quiet and soothing. He was about my height (five-foot-nine), but he was at least fifty pounds heavier.

If you have ever been in a hospital, you know the nursing and support staff perform virtually all of the routine care of the patients. Once I got to know Miguel I felt very confident in his abilities because I learned he had received some training in medical school. He wasn't just any old helping hand hired off the street; he knew what he was doing.

When I was transferred from the intensive care unit to the orthopedic wing where Miguel worked, I was in terrible pain (an understatement, given my twelve fractures), and I could not get settled into a comfortable position. I had new stitches from two operations that repaired internal problems, and I was facing three more operations in the next few weeks. I had one leg in traction and my other leg and right arm in a sling. An oxygen mask covered my face.

That was my situation when Miguel introduced himself and told me it would be his job to keep me as comfortable as possible. The look in his eyes told me he meant it. He helped me shave and keep clean, he made sure I had food and drink, and he kept ice nearby and applied it to my forehead in a cold compress to ease my fever.

It is hard to relate the kind of pain I felt, particularly in the first three or four weeks, because it was so strong and constant. Family members and other visitors would express sympathy and encouragement, but I knew Miguel understood best what I was going through.

My confidence in him came from his knack for anticipating my needs. I could not walk, but as my healing progressed I was allowed to ride in a reclining wheelchair. (We called it "the Cadillac.") Each time I was lifted into the Cadillac, Miguel was there to put pillows under my knees to absorb any blows and to keep undue pressure off my legs. It was a small gesture, I know, but he didn't have to be told to do it. Such gestures made me appreciate him all the more.

Once when we were alone in my room, I told him, "Miguel, I don't think I've ever known anyone who could feel another person's hurts the way you do. I really appreciate that."

"It's a very simple matter," he explained. "I've never had broken legs, but I try to think each time I help you what I might want if I did. Then I do that for you." His voice was so calm and matter-of-fact he made his thoughtfulness sound routine, but I knew how unique Miguel was.

"Miguel, I've been told you were once in training to enter medical school, but after leaving your country you had to give up that dream, at least for the time being. Does it ever frustrate you to work as an orderly instead of as a doctor?"

"Oh, no, not at all. I don't mind if I'm not the one performing surgery or giving the medical advice. All I want to do is be on the front lines somewhere, helping. It doesn't matter who does what job; we're all part of the team."

That attitude sure is different from what we normally see in America. Most of us aspire to get away from the more menial tasks and aim for the glory position. But Miguel didn't care which rung of the ladder he was standing on; he was just glad to be on the ladder.

My experiences and observations with Miguel prompted me to think about my own life. I asked myself, *How willing am I to do menial tasks? What if someone else gets the credit for what I do?*

Miguel's attitude made me see myself as being more self-centered than I wanted to admit. All sorts of examples of my self-preoccupation popped into my mind: my tendency to interrupt others in conversation, my impatience, my tuning others out. I wanted to be less like the "me-first" person I was and more like Miguel.

Have you ever examined your inclination to be preoccupied with yourself, your own thoughts and needs? Self-preoccupation doesn't always present itself in the glaringly obvious form of arrogance. It also occurs in many common daily circumstances. Can you relate to any of the following scenarios?

- Your spouse does not speak in the tone of voice you like, so you respond in a less-than-wonderful manner too.
- Your child ignores your request for help, so you speak in an abrupt fashion.
- As you hear a friend talk about wonderful family

times, you inwardly question, *Why don't I ever have the same good fortune?*

Don't feel odd if you tend to be self-preoccupied. We all are! Notice the behavior of an eighteen-month-old child. He is tuned in to his own little world. When he gets his way, he is happy; when he doesn't, he cries. It's as simple as that. The young child is demonstrating the self-centered core of human nature. As the child grows older, he will shed some of the baser aspects of this trait, but a remnant will always remain. This is because we are each "in Adam."

We develop humility as we resist self-centeredness and acknowledge we are not the center of the universe. In humility we understand that life is not obliged to fall in line with our personal preferences, and though we may sometimes assert those preferences, we will not demand that others follow them.

I asked Miguel to tell me about life back in Nicaragua, and he chuckled as he said, "It's very different there. Here, you have so many things you just want more. There, you don't have much so you appreciate anything you have."

He told me he was the son of a common laborer who worked odd jobs, mostly in the construction business, to support his wife and six children. "We never knew we were poor because no one else in our neighborhood had any more than we did," he said.

Miguel excelled in school, so he was encouraged to continue his education after his siblings quit. Nonetheless, he never wanted to be accused of not pulling his weight at home, so from an early age he would pick up odd jobs in town just as his brothers and sisters did. "We all pooled our money together, and as a family we never lacked."

That pull-together attitude kept Miguel from being too consumed with his own self. Not that he did not take care of himself, but he was not preoccupied with the idea.

In his late teens, Miguel was given the opportunity to work at a small local hospital, assisting in virtually every aspect of patient care, from working in the operating rooms to helping in the minor emergency rooms. "We had trained doctors who supervised our work, but we were each expected to know all the jobs because there was no way of predicting who would be needed at any given time for some procedure. If a bed needed to be made, you did it. If the doctor needed assistance in surgery, you did that too."

Miguel knew that everyone benefited when each person set aside his or her own ego for the good of the group. I liked that attitude, and I knew I could learn from him. One thing Miguel taught me was that God can use a person, even with less than perfect skills, if he or she has the right heart.

Humility means we are genuinely willing to be used by God in whatever role He places in front of us. Rather than worrying about situations with a "what's-in-it-for-me?" attitude, in humility we look at the big picture first, taking into account everyone's needs.

Looking back, I realized I learned some much-needed lessons in humility as I lay flat on my back for eight weeks. I would never have dreamed that the hospital would be a classroom, and I surely would not have guessed that an orderly named Miguel would be a master professor. Nonetheless, there he was, with his history of broken plans and education, taking me to school—me, the guy with all the degrees but nowhere near the application that humble Miguel had.

In addition to giving up my self-centeredness, to be humble I must also recognize my limits.

Acknowledging Limits

Common sense tells us we cannot control our world. I simply cannot get inside your mind and make you think the way I do. I cannot force a child to appreciate my wisdom. I cannot always be in control of my emotions, although I try. I'm limited. My humanness, by definition, keeps me from having godlike abilities.

When pride kicks into gear, it throws out such common sense. I ignore reality and seek to live as if my ability to control were unlimited. For instance, pride can cause us to sulk in disbelief when we realize another person chooses to reject us; or it can cause us to be critical of others' differences, as if they are obliged to live *our* way.

I learned that Miguel had fled to America with his family for political asylum. Somehow they were known in Nicaragua to be unsympathetic to the communistic military regime that was strangling the country's political structure, so their options were either to leave or to stay and face potential death. Before he fled, Miguel was enrolled in premed courses, but all that had to be left behind.

I had already completed my graduate training by the time of my accident, and I naturally asked myself, *How might I fare if I had to abruptly leave my career goals behind and flee to an unknown country?* The thought of it boggled my mind. So one evening when his workload was slow, I asked Miguel again, "Doesn't it drive you crazy that you couldn't complete your plans for medical school?"

"Why should it?"

Come again? It seemed to me that *anyone* could understand my questioning. I know I'd have fought bitterness and disillusionment if the same thing had happened to me. At the very least, I'm sure I would have chronically played the "what if?" game over and over in my mind.

"I had no ability to control the communist uprising in my country," Miguel patiently explained. "It's true the communists have ruined my homeland, but I am just one man. I could not force the social scene to go my way. I *wanted* to take my stand and fight back, but the family decided together that we must seek freedom while we could. I try not to worry about the things I cannot control."

All my life I had been taught to take charge of as much of my world as I possibly could. And while some of that was good, I'm certain I had crossed a line from responsibility into pride. Miguel certainly missed his hometown and his friends. He was on a very different life path than he would have ever guessed. Yet he genuinely was not angry. In fact, he seemed content.

Are you like me? Do you have trouble accepting your limits?

Even God places limits on Himself in His interactions with others (at least for now). Jesus spoke with authority, but He did not often use the ramrod approach. He dearly desired to lead individuals into successful habits, yet He recognized the refusal of some to be led.

Consider some of the implications in your life as you live humbly within your own limits:

- Instead of insisting that you appear perfect, you can unashamedly let others see how you still need growth.
- If someone confronts you about a problem, you can listen without defending yourself.
- When you confront someone, you can be mindful that he or she may hold an equally legitimate viewpoint.

When you are aware of your own limits, you experience both freedom and strength: freedom because you do not have to be superhuman and strength because you can be composed when life does not unfold precisely as you would like.

Once I give up my self-centeredness and acknowledge my limits, I am able to have a bondservant's heart.

Adopting the Heart of a Bondservant

In Paul's sermon on humility, he described Jesus as "taking the form of a bondservant." Though the word *bondservant* is not common today, the term gives us a rich insight into Christ's humility.

In the days of Roman rule, a master could free a slave by providing the necessary papers that stated the person would no longer be bound as a slave; he or she was free.

But sometimes this newly freed person would tell his or her master: "Though I am free to do what I choose, I wish to remain with you as your servant. I will continue to act as a slave though we both know I am not one." This was a bondservant.

Jesus maintained this bondservant's mind-set, first in His devotion to God, then in His commitments to people. Though He had the capability to do whatever He wanted whenever He wanted, He chose to be the free servant of those who needed Him. In doing so, He set aside His self-preoccupations, preferring instead to be preoccupied with those He loved.

I admit that a bondservant's attitude can be difficult to achieve in various situations. Perhaps a husband wants his wife to respect him more so he thinks, *If I'm her servant, she may just take advantage of my good nature. I've got to show her who's boss.* A mother may wonder, *I serve my children all day long. When do I get a break?* A supervisor at work thinks, *If I'm too easy on my employees, they'll be less productive.* A friend believes, *Everyone knows I'm good natured, so they constantly ask me to do more than I'm capable of.*

Have you ever entertained similar thoughts? I know I have. There is always the possibility that someone will misuse us. That's why, in our black-and-white thinking, we reason, *Servitude creates problems, so forget it!*

Not so fast! Yes, servitude can invite people to be insensitive. (I'm sure Jesus received many annoying requests and demands from people who wanted one more favor from Him.) Yet we cannot be all things to all people.

A good example comes from Jesus' interaction with His

disciples the night before His arrest. When it was time to clean up before the Passover meal, custom required that a younger or lesser member of the group take a basin of water to wash the feet of those present. As the leader, Jesus was in the position to assign this task to one of the men. Yet quietly, with no words, He stripped to His undergarments, took the basin, and unbegrudgingly performed this inglorious task.

Why did He do this? To communicate the powerful message: Our God is a serving God.

As I got to know Miguel, I kept a close eye on him to determine if he was consistent in his attitudes. He usually came into my room when the doctors were tending to me, and I noticed his solid rapport with them. He seemed to clearly anticipate their requests, which told me he could put himself in their shoes too. But then I noticed he had the same steadiness and eagerness to help when it came to doing the most menial tasks, like helping me use the bathroom or giving me a bath.

When I asked him once, "Miguel, do you ever get tired of what you have to do around here?" his response showed me his heart. He said, "I suppose if I *had* to do these things I would get tired of it, but I choose to do what I do."

"Even emptying bedpans?"

He grinned (and I was glad to know he was human), "Well, that's not exactly the most glamorous part, but aren't there parts of everyone's work that are less than perfect?"

This spirit of servitude is reserved primarily for those who have the maturity to understand that their greatness is found in such simplicity. Think of times when we are called upon to use power and could, instead, embrace the servant's role.

For example, a mother who is required to make many sacrifices each day on her child's behalf could go through the monotonous routine begrudgingly; instead she shows her pleasure in helping the child, and by her actions and her attitude she teaches her child kindness and consideration.

A husband embraces the servant's role when he acknowledges his position as head of the household but does not use this position to be the boss. Instead, he considers how he can help his wife and children feel special, and he is willing to be a leader by helping in menial household tasks.

In the workplace, the supervisor who aspires to the servant's role works to be an uplifting presence for his or her employees rather than being a demanding taskmaster. The servant-supervisor knows that the best way to motivate others is through encouragement.

I'll have to admit that prior to knowing Miguel, I thought of humility as lying down and letting people wipe their feet on me. But I was wrong, very wrong. In humility is strength.

CAN HUMBLE PEOPLE ALSO BE FORCEFUL?

During my hospital stay, a student nurse was part of the team on my ward. One morning this young lady was changing a bandage on my broken arm when Miguel walked in. Recognizing that she was being, shall we say, less than delicate in handling my wound, Miguel stepped in and instructed her in the more appropriate procedure. He praised her for the effort she was making at the same time he showed her how to improve her technique.

After she left the room I smiled up at him and said, "Thanks for rescuing me. She'd have had me screaming for mercy if you had not intervened!" We both laughed.

"Well, there are times when you just have to take charge, but you've got to do it without insulting the person," Miguel said. Then he quietly added, "She's learning."

I thought to myself, *Lord, You know I don't like lying here with all these broken bones, but You also know how much I needed to know a guy like Miguel. Thanks for putting him in my path.*

As we communicate strong opinions, we need to maintain respect and empathy. While others need our input, they also need us to acknowledge their worth. This delicate balance means when we discipline our children, we simultaneously want them to know we love them. When we reprimand an employee, we are also aware that he or she has probably seen many of our own imperfect work practices too. When we are in a dispute with our mate we show willingness to listen to his or her viewpoint as we speak our own.

And how will people respond to us if we act humbly? Again, let's look to our Lord's life for a parallel.

THE PEOPLE'S RESPONSE TO JESUS

Many times people responded to Jesus' humility the way we think they should have: with awe and admiration.

When the shepherds saw Him in His humble beginnings, they praised God and worshiped Him. When Jesus ministered to hordes of people, healing them and teaching new truths of grace and forgiveness, the crowds loved Him and begged for more. Humility has a way of bringing out the best in people.

And the worst.

While Jesus won the hearts of a centurion and a fellow sufferer on the cross, the soldiers and the Jews scorned and ridiculed Him. While the wise men sought Him for worship, King Herod plotted to kill Him. While eleven disciples honored Him as Lord, one consorted with His adversaries.

Some people are repulsed by holiness. Power-hungry persons may prey upon a person's good nature. But our humility cannot be contingent upon others' responses. We adopt it because it is central to God's character and for that reason alone, worthy of our focus.

I was able to thank Miguel for all he had done for me, both during my stay at the hospital and afterward. For a year I had to use a cane to walk around, and I have had to undergo a little more surgical work, mostly on my knees. But I've recovered from my injuries now, at least to the extent that I carry on a normal life.

One Saturday evening, I received word that a friend had been admitted to the hospital unexpectedly, so I went to the friend's room to comfort him. Guess who the orderly was on his floor! Miguel. Thirteen years after I had met him, he still had not lost those extra fifty pounds, and his hair was a lot grayer, but he was as busy serving my friend as he had served me.

Because it had been so many years since we had seen each other (and I had spent most of our time together flat on my back in hospital gowns), I couldn't help but ask him, "Hey, Miguel, do you remember me?"

He looked intently at my face, then broke into a wide smile. "Yeah, the guy who can't water-ski worth a flip!" He hugged my neck, and it sure felt good.

I told him how much his care and attention had meant to me at a time when I needed an extra dose of kindness. "I wish I knew how to say thank you in a more elaborate way," I said, "but words are the best I can do at the moment."

Like Miguel, Jesus was a refugee of sorts, leaving His home in heaven and the grandness of God's throne to willingly become a servant who brought healing to my soul, which was broken and infected by pride. Just as I was reunited with Miguel, I will someday be reunited with Jesus, but I will have an eternity to tell Him thank you. And I will be joined by those myriads of others who will do the same. What an eternity it will be!

In the meantime, thank you, Miguel, for showing me just a glimpse of Jesus' humility.

— 3 —

His Self-Restraint:

The Temptation in the Wilderness

Matthew 4:1–11

I once had a conversation with a woman about the irritations of parenting. When she explained how she frustrated herself by being impatient, I responded with a knowing nod, saying that I felt that same self-directed frustration when I snapped impatiently at my kids.

Her eyes grew big as she said, "*You* have snapped at your children?"

I chuckled as I thought, *If you're surprised by that simple revelation, I'd hate to have to tell you about some of my other sins!*

As I reflected on this interchange later, it occurred to me that we Christians put heavy pressure on one another to be superhuman. We dislike admitting that a growing, mature Christian can actually struggle with the same problems as non-Christians. This feeds an unhealthy tendency for Christians to hide their humanness in the false hope that they can somehow fool others into thinking they are beyond common pitfalls and temptations. Ultimately, this practice is an unhealthy reinforcer of phoniness and hypocrisy.

So let's be open in admitting that we each struggle against our own self-will. Speaking for myself, I know what it is like to envy another person's success. I have also contended with resentment, clinging to anger beyond the point of appropriateness. I am familiar with lust, having allowed my mind to dwell on sexual curiosities. And I have been tempted to portray myself in a favorable light that would falsely cover my ineptitudes.

Are you surprised? I hope not. I am merely admitting the same human tendencies all sinners experience. If you have not had the same temptations as I have (or vice versa) it is only because we differ in our personalities and our circumstances. We each live in Satan's domain, and we can be assured that he will try to lure us away from God.

SATAN'S ENTICEMENTS

I do not know the mechanics Satan uses to produce temptation, except that he entices our minds to dwell on thoughts that feed egotistical cravings. Satan launches attacks through our innermost thoughts and desires to render us impotent as agents of God.

In years past, I commanded myself to no longer have tempting urges. If I could be rid of these intrusions, I reasoned, I would be home free. But after laboring under the extra burden of guilt that ensued, I revised my self-talk. I admitted that I could not keep Satan from pursuing me with many temptations but I *could* practice self-restraint as each one occurred. That seemed more reasonable and workable.

How skilled are you in the trait of self-restraint? If you are like most of us, you succeed quite nicely in some areas while falling flat on your face in others. You may show great discipline in managing your time at work while you struggle with the need to push away from the dinner table before overindulging. Perhaps you can control your temper around your neighbors but you are prone to emotional outbursts with your spouse.

Jesus is the standard-bearer for self-restraint. In His humanity He experienced temptation, but He was so yielded to God, He mastered all temptation to do wrong. He proved to be a more than worthy adversary to Satan, and He can enable you and me to be the same.

By about age thirty, Jesus was prompted by God to inaugurate His ministry. But first, He knew He needed time alone to pray and plan and meditate on how He would implement God's perfect will. He chose to retreat to the wilderness, probably the area of southern Israel between Jerusalem and the Dead Sea, rather than taking a relaxing vacation along the Mediterranean shore. Stretching over an area of thirty-five by fifteen miles, this place was once called *Jeshimon,* meaning "the Devastation." Draped with yellow sand and limestone, the area was bare and rugged, sparsely populated, and known for its blistering heat and lack of vegetation.

Why did Jesus choose such an unappealing landscape to collect His thoughts? Because He knew that there He could gather His resolve by freeing Himself of the comforts that so easily soften a young minister's burning mission to please God. He wanted, He needed, to be away from any outside distraction, and the Devastation offered the likeliest place. By selecting the Devastation, Jesus illustrated a core quality necessary for self-restraint: a preference for simplicity.

Whenever Satan thinks he has an opportunity to bring havoc to one seeking God, he will seize the moment. Waiting until the end of Jesus' time alone, he approached Christ with the same powerful temptations he uses on you and me today.

No doubt, after almost six weeks in the wilderness, Jesus was physically and emotionally ready to return home. Satan concluded that in His weariness, Jesus would be more susceptible to outside suggestion. That's when he approached Jesus.

One of Satan's common ploys is to strike when we are in an emotionally weakened state. Have you noticed how temptation occurs more powerfully when you are physically or emotionally tired? Or when you feel rejected? Or when you are away from those you love? Satan delights in pulling us further into the pit when we are already a bit down.

The first temptation was to turn stones into bread. The desert contained many small round rocks shaped like loaves of bread, so the visual imagery worked well in Satan's seduction. Being human, Jesus' stomach growled just like yours or mine, so surely He would listen to the logic that He should miraculously conjure up some bread.

But with laser-sharp insight, the Lord realized something more was at stake. He knew He was being encouraged to use His God-given capabilities for a selfish pursuit, and He understood that His miracle-working powers were to be used only to show God's presence in His life. So, seeing through Satan's ploy, He resisted the urge to be self-serving. His response to Satan reflected this understanding: "It is written, 'Man shall not live by bread alone, but by every word that proceeds from the mouth of God'" (Matt. 4:4). He practiced self-restraint.

How have you been tempted to selfishly pursue your own needs even if it means ignoring God's intentions for you? Each of your skills, you know, can be used for selfish gain. You may have a winsome personality but, instead of using it to be an encourager, you may use it to get your own way. Or perhaps you have strong organizational skills but, instead of helping others with those skills, you are inclined to be regimented and critical. Each positive characteristic can have its negative downside, and Satan is most pleased when we use what might be good in a perverse way. Jesus was wise enough to recognize and avoid this trap.

Not satisfied with Jesus' resistance, Satan pressed further. He took Jesus to the pinnacle of the temple and tempted Him to jump down and allow the angels to catch Him in midair, thereby creating an amazing scene that would attract a great number of followers. Then, to add credibility to his suggestion, Satan quoted Scripture, albeit out of context, reminding Jesus that God would give the angels charge over His concerns.

This second temptation was an enticement to use sensation and titillation to generate popular appeal. Surely, Satan reasoned, Jesus could use the notoriety to begin His public ministry. After all, what common person would reject someone who could perform such spectacular public displays?

Satan knows people can be swayed by superficial appeals. In a like manner, he tempts you and me to create appealing but superficial impressions to gain public approval. Have you ever portrayed yourself as being more "together" or more successful than you really are? Popularity and acceptance are so important that we can willingly succumb to the temptation to create illusions about ourselves.

Jesus was in complete command of all creation, so a simple feat like leaping from a building would have been child's play for Him. But again, He recognized that a deeper issue was at stake. If He drew people to Him only through signs and wonders, His followers would want to see more and more, which would eventually lead them to a superficial belief. Jesus, in fact, *would* perform some miracles that would establish Him as One sent from God, but He wanted His reputation to be anchored more in His compassion and His humility than in His miraculous power. Unlike sensational events, the qualities of compassion and humility were lasting.

Rejecting Satan's temptation and resisting the allure of popular acclaim at the expense of an authentic, relationship-based appeal, Jesus quoted Scripture to explain that it is irreverent to test God. He told Satan, "It is written . . . 'You shall not tempt the LORD your God'" (Matt. 4:7). He practiced self-restraint.

Not one to take no for an answer, Satan approached Jesus with a third temptation. Showing Jesus the kingdoms of the world, Satan promised Jesus if He would worship him, Jesus could have all the world had to offer. In essence, he was communicating: *Ease up on Your high and lofty standards, Jesus. Loosen Your demands, and You'll find that more people will like You and follow You.*

You and I are bombarded with this temptation each day through advertising messages, through worldly-minded acquaintances, through relatives and friends with lax principles. We are encouraged to view traditional Christian sexual values as old-fashioned and out of sync with the times. We are encouraged to put material gain before personal integrity. We have learned that the seriousness of lying can be softened by humorously calling it "fudging the truth."

Jesus knew He could not change the world by becoming like the world. So focused was He in His mission for God that He resisted the appeal to compromise. His refusal to succumb to this temptation was not born out of contempt for the world but from compassion for those hurting from the effects of ungodliness. He knew how desperately these people needed to encounter God, so He quoted to Satan a Scripture instructing us to worship and serve God alone: "Away with you, Satan! For it is written, 'You shall worship the LORD your God, and Him only you shall serve'" (Matt. 4:10). Peace is found only in an ongoing relationship with Him.

These three temptations represent the major enticements that lure you and me away from God: self-indulgence, superficial appeals for acceptance, and compromise. In His humanness, Christ determined that the only way to be truly representative of God was to resist the temporary attractiveness of these temptations. He knew that godliness requires self-restraint, which prompts us to consider God's eternal goodness over mankind's temporary pleasure.

Dick, a fifty-one-year-old man, was questioning many of the teachings that had driven him to perform correctly for years. "I can see that I've excelled at pleasing people and living according to the correct formulas for life, but right now I'm increasingly weary of having to fit the mold. I'm tired of setting aside my preferences because of someone else's preferences. It's time for me to cut loose and be my own person, even if it means others might be displeased."

I was aware that Dick's wife, Shelly, believed Dick was in the midst of a mid-life crisis and was very vulnerable to any temptation that would lead him away from his traditional values. While Dick initially spoke to me with an edge of rebellion, he also demonstrated uncertainty and insecurity and defensiveness. So I asked him to talk with me about the temptations that had put him in his current emotional turmoil.

"Never before have I allowed myself to think about being with any woman other than my wife, but right now a change of pace would be pretty appealing," he said. "In the past, I've never let myself get very frustrated, but nowadays I'm frustrated at every turn. I have friends who have a much looser lifestyle, and I've been thinking that I'd like a taste of their freedom."

He went on to explain that he was joining co-workers in after-work happy hours at nearby bars and was enjoying the atmosphere there.

"Part of me knows I've got to be careful not to stray too far from my conservative roots," he said, "but another part of me doesn't care. I'm aware that this is how many men become ensnared by affairs or alcoholism, but I go back and forth, trying to decide what camp I want to be in."

RESISTING TEMPTATION

What temptations do you struggle with? Notice my question. I did not ask if you ever struggle with temptations, because I know you do. I'm asking which temptations are common to you. You may be tempted, like Dick, to seek out what the party crowd describes as the good life. Perhaps you struggle with secret sexual fantasies. Maybe you have a hard time saving money. Or perhaps you have strong emotional struggles with anger or jealousy that keep you wrapped up in an inner tug-of-war. Like the rest of us, you have your vulnerable spots.

You cannot dictate what feelings or circumstances you will encounter each day. Many times you will be exposed to alternative viewpoints or lifestyles by chance, simply because you encounter someone who openly displays something different. Or others may openly invite you to join them in behaviors that will clearly lead you away from your philosophical roots. Whatever the case, be on guard against the temptations that can most easily pull you into behavior that is counter to healthy living.

To practice the self-restraint needed to resist temptations, consider the following suggestions.

Accept the Inevitable

Many people feel excessively guilty when they are tempted. If they envy another's success, they think: *I can't believe I am jealous of my friend Joe's (or Mary's) good fortune.* Or if they experience thoughts of lustful fantasy they may reason: *I'm lower than low because I have indulged wrong thoughts.*

This self-deprecating pattern leads to another bad habit: forcing purity upon ourselves to the point that we don't accept our personal frailties. Dick told me, "Ever since I was a teenager I've been lectured about the evils of sexual thoughts. I've tried and tried to avoid them, but now I'm ready to give up on it. My thoughts always seem to wander in the wrong direction."

Dick had put so much pressure on himself he was on the verge of letting the temptation run its full course.

In His great Sermon on the Mount, Jesus shared two ideas that have been seriously misconstrued by many people like Dick. He said if you cling to lust in your heart it is equal to being adulterous, and if you harbor hateful anger it is analogous to being a murderer. Many have taken this to mean that we are never to lust or hate if we are good Christians.

But Jesus' words were not instructions; they were descriptions. Speaking to people who thought they could work their way into righteousness, He was saying, in effect, "Even if you have never committed adultery or murder, I want you to be honest about what is truly in your mind. You indulge lustful thoughts as well as hateful thoughts; that is part of what you are as sinners. As you admit this truth, you can more readily acknowledge how desperately you need a Savior."

I remember my own reaction when I first became aware of Christ's words about lust and hate. In my devout commitment to the Lord, I was determined to cease from having any stray thoughts or feelings. Of course, this made me a sitting duck waiting to be struck by guilt. It also made me feel that I would never measure up to such lofty standards, meaning I would eventually learn to resent Christian principles because of their impossibility.

But in time I realized how wrong my interpretation of Christ's words were. A major theme throughout His teaching is our complete and total inability to present ourselves in perfect stead before God. The Old Testament law had one major purpose: to show us performance-minded people just how inept we are in our capacity to live correctly.

When I learned to admit (both to myself and to others) that I was part of this imperfect world, that I could never come close to God's lofty standards, I felt free then to realistically pursue my options when faced with temptations.

We *will* lust. We *will* indulge in inappropriate anger. These are undeniable facts of human nature. When we pretend to live as if we will never have such inner struggles, we only kid ourselves and cause increased emotional tension.

A crucial first step to developing self-restraint is to admit that we will never be immune to temptation. Another step is being open about our temptations.

Be Open about Your Temptations

Once you accept the certainty of temptation, you can move to a higher realm by openly confessing those temptations to mature and responsible friends. The Bible offers many "one another" instructions (confess to one another, love one another, forgive one another, and so on), implying our need to be linked together. The most ignored of these instructions is to bear one another's burdens. We prefer to pretend we do not have burdens, so we agonizingly carry them alone, refusing to let others see what we really are. This habit only causes the temptations to gain a more powerful hold on us.

You have surely been in a Christian prayer group when the leader asks for prayer requests and the usual requests are made, asking others to pray for a sick relative or for a friend who lost a job. But how often does someone say, "Pray for me as I struggle with my greed"? Or, "I have a bad temper, and I'm in need of healing in this area"?

Instead we live with increasing difficulty in the areas that need the greatest attention from those who love us.

Realizing this as one of Dick's needs, I told him, "No wonder you want something different. I'd want to be free, too, of a system that offered conditional acceptance and judgment."

We proceeded to discuss how he needed a new lease on life, but it did not have to be anchored in secular living. I urged him to fuse his craving for a different life with his understanding that godliness is an appropriate lifestyle.

"I wonder if you can set a new pattern into motion with your friends and family members. Rather than being irresponsibly rebellious, be a trendsetter by coming out into the open about your real needs and hurts and struggles. Let folks see the real you, even if it is not flattering. By being open you will feel less of a craving to run wild."

Self-restraint is made possible by wide-open honesty. As you clearly reveal your problems to people you trust, you will find a growing sense of accountability. Sharing your real self creates bonding with others, which is an important ingredient in personal growth. Take the example of the apostle Paul, who openly confessed his own struggles in this area, saying, "The good that I will to do, I do not do; but the evil I will not to do, that I practice" (Rom. 7:19). Paul said he struggled to do what was right because he was repeatedly drawn toward things he knew were wrong. Paradoxically, though, by making his confession he was less inclined to act upon his sinful impulses. His admission caused him to clearly recognize that whatever course he followed was a matter of choice.

Dick later told me, "I took you up on your advice to be open with a friend, and it paid good dividends. I told a man at work that I felt tempted to pursue a more worldly lifestyle than my Christian values would allow, and he readily agreed that this was, indeed, a real option for me. But then he shared some of the pain he had put himself through a few years ago by seeking selfish pleasure. It's odd, but once I exposed my feelings to someone I respected, my craving to stray diminished."

Most temptations are appealing because of fantasies of bliss associated with them. But open disclosure has a way of revealing the illusions in our desires. Self-restraint then becomes less of an issue of begrudging obligation and more a reasonable choice.

Think of times when you could find reasonable restraint through self-disclosure. You may need to confess to a person or group the struggles you have with overeating or alcohol abuse or failure to control your anger. Perhaps you can talk honestly with your teen about your need to be more fair-minded in disciplinary matters. Or you might admit to your spouse that you have insecurities that need to be tenderly nurtured.

As we consider the temptations affecting our lives, we need to also reflect on the pros and cons we would encounter if we experimented with different behavior.

View Experimentation As Both Good and Risky

In one of my sessions with Dick, he told me, "I must confess that I had reservations about this counseling because you are a Christian. My struggles are definitely not consistent with Christian values, so I figured you would be hard on me. But instead you have accepted me, and I am pleasantly surprised."

A quick thought ran through my mind: *How sad that a person is surprised when a Christian chooses to be evenhanded.* I spoke openly with him and said, "I'm aware that you won't make your adjustments if I just tell you what to do. You need someone to give you the room to experiment with your ideas. Even though this may be potentially risky, you'll not arrive at solid life patterns until you explore your choices, both wise and unwise."

Shaking his head, he said, "I'm not sure I'll like what comes from me. I mean, lately I've thought a lot about just going with the flow of what I feel at the moment."

Temptation can cause a person to question the validity of well-taught values, so it can, indeed, wear down his or her resolve to live right. But if handled maturely, temptation can cause a person to become a deeper thinker who sorts through his or her personal priorities and eventually recognizes and clings to the values that are God-inspired. I explained to Dick, "In the past you've had decent lifestyle habits, but you apparently performed them only out of a sense of duty. So let's declare you a free agent who will question the validity of anything you've been taught. Are you game?"

Smiling, he asked, "What would this entail?"

"Let's take a simple instruction you've heard all your life . . . that you should be respectful to others. At this point, you may decide that this rule is for the birds, that respect is a sissy way of life. Instead of being respectful, you will be committed to rudeness."

"Well, I wouldn't want to be rude everywhere I go," he protested. "That wouldn't make any sense."

"Okay, you may decide that it makes no sense to indulge the temptation to be rude or condescending to others, but this decision needs to be your choice, not someone else's mandate."

We continued by examining his preferences regarding several other subjects such as moral purity, drunkenness, financial responsibility, and commitment to family. I explained that he could, in fact, experiment with each of these lifestyle issues in whatever way he wanted. But I also reminded him, "As you consider these options, you'd better factor in the consequences of your choices."

Too often Christians like to pretend they have no compelling feeling to look at the raw side of life. But in fact, we each have experienced enticements that cause us to wonder if it would be more pleasurable to abandon traditional values in favor of looser standards. So let's be honest; we *can* allow harsh anger to dominate, we *can* be immoral, we *can* be apathetic.

Persons who practice self-restraint don't deny these options. They have carefully determined that patience and servitude and tolerance, the characteristics of restraint, are what they genuinely want. The risk of choosing the opposites is too costly. Questioning and considering the pros and cons of different behavior are not the same as being committed to that behavior. By choosing not to act upon the evil, our preference for good is more deeply rooted.

Using Scripture as a guide can help you hold fast to this choice.

Seek Scriptural Guidance

Each time Satan tempted Jesus, he was met with a response from Scripture. Even when Satan attempted to beat Jesus at this game by misrepresenting a scriptural passage, Jesus held firmly to His commitment to God's Word. Jesus withstood any invitation to self-serving enticements because He knew God's objective truth.

Do you know Scripture? I did not ask if you know many of the Bible's stories. What I mean is, do you comprehend the logic of the Bible's message? Do you yearn to know it more deeply as each year passes and as your life experiences broaden?

Many people who succumb to self-indulging behaviors do so with a full knowledge that they contradict Scripture. For instance, a man may repeatedly give in to temperamental outbursts in spite of his awareness of the instruction to be kind. Or a woman may succumb to the craving to overeat even though she has been taught that her body is to be cared for as a temple of the Holy Spirit.

These behaviors are often practiced in direct defiance of Scripture because Scripture has been presented only as a religious book of do's and don'ts. Instead, Scripture needs to be a guide that we dearly respect.

Dick admitted, "I've seen many other people enjoy the benefits of a looser lifestyle than mine, and I've always refrained from going along because it was against my religion. It's gotten to the point that I resent my religion because it is so restrictive."

He was somewhat surprised when I said, "I'd resent teachings, too, if they only served to stymie my real beliefs. You don't need a religion that suffocates you."

Then I added, "I've become wary of my own impulses and of the world's enticements to the extent that I genuinely *want* a good code of living, and I've found the Bible to be that code. But you'll have to decide for yourself if it can be your code too."

Do you consider Scripture merely someone else's rules imposed on you? If so, you may decide to rethink your reason for following its ways. Be willing to question why you would choose its philosophies over worldly ideas. As you read it, think how you can apply it to your practical circumstances.

Jesus clearly chose not to give in to personal impulses because He knew it would be counter to Scripture's well-laid plans. But there is never any evidence that He deferred to Scripture begrudgingly. He so yearned to live for God and to do His will that it was a delight to comply with His instructions.

Think about the many biblical instructions that imply the need for self-restraint. Do you *really* believe in them?

- "Flee sexual immorality," says 1 Corinthians 6:18. Do you desire to be morally pure because you agree that it is better to consider long-term consequences over short-term pleasure?

- James 3:8 says, "No man can tame the tongue. It is an unruly evil, full of deadly poison." Can you corral your sharp tongue because you want to be known as a loving person?
- Ephesians 4:25 says that we are to speak truth with each other, "for we are members of one another." Can you refrain from name-calling when you are irritated, choosing instead to be respectful?
- Paul says, "Let nothing be done through selfish ambition or conceit, but in lowliness of mind let each esteem others better than himself" (Phil. 2:3). Can you put others' needs before your own, knowing this is consistent with humility?

Applying scriptural truths requires that you not only realize that God's ways are right and good, but that you genuinely crave to have them in the center of your life.

This craving for scriptural guidelines is not a one-time decision. It is a need that continues as long as we live.

THE CONTINUING NEED FOR SELF-RESTRAINT

Jesus was able to respond resolutely to Satan's temptations because He knew the attacks were inevitable, because He carefully thought through His responses, and because He deliberately chose to follow the guidelines of Scripture. For a time after the temptations, Satan left Jesus, and the Lord was comforted by the angels. But we know

Satan did not let up on his attack upon Christ. In fact, Satan's evil work continues to this day as he attempts to entice Christ's followers—you and me—away from the path to salvation.

We can be assured that these attacks will continue; inevitably, temptations will be an ongoing presence in all of our lives. They can come from family members, from the media, from neighbors, from within ourselves. But as we resist these temptations, as we follow Jesus' example and practice self-restraint, we defer to God's better alternatives for us. As a result, we find a peace of mind that's possible only with God.

His Kindness:

The Little Children Come to Him

Mark 10:13–16

A s a twenty-year-old college student in Waco, Texas, I had a job driving a school bus for a nearby elementary school. From the first day I saw Albert, I had him pegged as the chief troublemaker of the crowd. Most grade-school kids still have a vestige of respect for authority figures, so keeping most of my small passengers under control was no great problem. The lone exception was Albert.

Maybe it was the faded jeans I wore and the sweatshirts with the sleeves cut off, but Albert didn't see me as a person who would have any say in his life. Throwing spitballs, flicking girls on the ear, shouting, arguing—these were normal fare for this nine-year-old boy who never wore new clothes and whose curly black hair was always so rumpled it looked as if it never saw a comb. He was trouble, just looking for a place to happen.

I used up every technique I knew trying to get Albert to settle down. I'd pull the bus over and declare we would move again only when Albert became quiet. Peer pressure would surely get to him, I thought, and this usually worked for a time—but soon he'd forget the lesson. I'd make him sit in the seat directly behind the driver's chair, but that only meant torment for me. I'd bribe him with gum, but the other kids didn't take to that very well because they wanted some too.

If you have been in a similar situation with such a child, you know how your attention can stay riveted on that one troublemaker as you perpetually ask yourself, *What can I do to make him understand me?*

November came, and Waco had its first cold snap of the season. The boys and girls hustled to get onto the bus that afternoon, hurrying to get out of the cold and trying to get close to the big heater next to my oversized steering wheel. Albert was particularly cold because he was only wearing torn khakis and a dirty white T-shirt. He cursed the cold and said he hated winter.

As luck would have it (Why is it always this way?) Albert's stop was the last on my route. He was sitting

behind me, playing with my side stop signal, when I
asked, "Albert, did you leave your jacket at home this
morning?"

Defiantly he responded, "I don't have a jacket 'cause I
don't need one!"

I knew better. Those cold northern winds blowing
across central Texas that time of year served as solid
reminders that the summer heat wasn't such a bad thing
after all. (At least we could jump in the water, then, or
find activities indoors to cool us off.) No one wanted to
hang around outside when a winter northern blew
through. No matter how macho you were, that wind was
cold!

I turned back to face Albert. "You don't suppose your
mother would mind if you stayed on the bus and went
home with me this afternoon, would she?"

Albert's face lit up, and I knew he'd do anything to
keep from having to go home. I couldn't blame him. I'd
seen his drab wood-framed shack. Later I learned that
his mother, an illegal alien from Mexico, had lived there
with a succession of boyfriends, chronically worried
about how she would make ends meet for herself and
her four sons.

Would Albert go home with me? What a foolish question! Of course he would. After getting his mother's OK,
we made our way back to my modest rented house and
I told him we had an errand to run. Once in my car I said,
"Albert, in spite of your toughness I think you might
need a jacket this winter, so we're going to Kmart to find
something for you." Albert always tried hard to main-

tain his self-sufficient demeanor, but at that news he couldn't hold back. He burst out with a wide smile and asked, "Do you think—maybe—we could get a black one?"

I wasn't sure I had much padding in my personal budget for a new jacket, but I knew the little I had must look like a fortune to a scrawny little boy who had next to nothing.

We found the jackets in Kmart, and sure enough, there was a black bomber jacket with a fake-fur collar. "That's perfect! That's the one I want!" Albert shouted.

I told Albert he'd better get a size or two larger so it would last longer. Together we found just the right one, and shortly afterward he was marching out of that Kmart wearing his new merchandise like he was a Rockefeller. I'd never seen anyone so proud of anything in my entire life. And I was as happy as Albert.

It's funny, but Albert came into my life at a time when I was enamored by all the theories of psychology. I'd read the explanations for abnormal behavior, and I was conducting experiments to determine how to motivate people. I had to write papers on how the environment influences human behavior.

But right there on the school bus I was introduced to a sniveling, precocious nine-year-old boy who taught me every bit as much as my high-minded professors. I learned that authority and college degrees mean absolutely nothing without kindness. I realized how inept I was at explaining heavy-duty concepts like discipline to one who could not think in such lofty terms, yet I could show him

life-changing concepts by being kind and gentle—and
available.

CHRIST'S KINDNESS TO
LITTLE CHILDREN

Though Jesus had a powerful new message of grace and
redemption to share, He realized that a caring spirit would
be the ultimate way to carry that message into the hearts
of His listeners. He said, "If anyone thirsts, let him come
to Me and drink" (John 7:37).

Can't you just picture the inviting look on His face as
He spoke those words? His mission was to bring comfort
to those who had known rejection and judgment, and He
was determined that His demeanor would project the
compassion and understanding consistent with that mission. Kindness involves a nurturing, encouraging spirit.

Many illustrations could be used as a depiction of this
kindness, but none stand out quite like the time He openly
invited young children to surround Him, much to the
chagrin of His disciples. Well into His public ministry,
Jesus was a widely known teacher who attracted large
crowds wherever He went. Stories about His healings and
miracles had become legendary, and He had established
Himself as a talented communicator, set apart from the
routine assortment of itinerant teachers common in that
day.

After months of teaching in the northern regions of
Galilee, Jesus headed southeast to a territory beyond the

Jordan River known as Perea. Though He had not spent much time in the region, hordes of people stepped aside from the busyness of their schedules to hear Him teach and to be healed. As usual, the Pharisees followed closely, and whenever the chance arose they would lay philosophical traps, hoping to lead Jesus into a trumped-up controversy. Then, as soon as His formal talk had ended, and as the Pharisees were forced into retreat, the people would press near Him as they did wherever He went.

I can recall years ago when the president of the United States visited my university to give a lecture. There was standing room only as we crowded into the large auditorium. Soon the president's entourage of Secret Service agents and high officials made their way down the aisle near my seat. My heart raced at the prospect of being so close to such an important man. As the president passed me, a friend seated next to me extended his hand, and the president shook it and smiled warmly into his face. Can you imagine the special feeling that overcame my friend? His eyes twinkled brightly as he turned to the rest of us and proclaimed, "*I* got to shake hands with the president!"

Put yourself on that hillside two thousand years ago in Perea. Think for a moment how it might feel to be recognized by this Jesus, a man who had captured the hearts of an entire nation. Because of the prestige accompanying His fame, you would hope, *Perhaps I can be lucky enough to stand near Him or speak ever so briefly to Him or to touch Him.* What a privilege!

We do not know who had the idea first but some people, probably a group of mothers, felt compelled to take their young children to Jesus so He might bless them. They probably had to wait until the end of the day when the crowd was finally thinning out; yet these parents were willing to wait as long as necessary for their kids to have an audience with the Master.

In their culture, a blessing carried monumental importance. This laying on of hands was an open recognition of the individual's value, a powerful affirmation of his or her worth and importance to God, particularly when a man of Jesus' stature bestowed the blessing.

As the parents brought their children toward Jesus, His disciples were clearly annoyed. They believed children should be seen and not heard. (They would certainly feel uncomfortable with the 1990s style of catering to children and building an entire day around their entertainment needs!) They believed children should know that their place is *not* center stage. So they scolded the parents, shooing them away and telling them to leave. Jesus had no time for their petty request, they said.

Boy, were they wrong! The Gospel writer, Mark, recorded that Jesus was indignant at the sight of His disciples' actions. How could the disciples have had so much exposure to Him yet be so unaware of His tender feelings for little ones? He had been in their homes and played with their sons and daughters and nieces and nephews. They had seen Him patiently receive "just one more" request many times. And they had felt His kindness personally. Were they *this* dense?

Firmly but patiently, in a voice that would not scare the children, Jesus said, "Let the little children come to Me."

Now imagine how the children, who may have been anywhere from toddlers to preteens, responded to this invitation. We do not know how many there were, perhaps a dozen, maybe more. Undoubtedly, they rushed to the ground where He sat, His arms opened wide. Imagine Jesus smiling as He hugged the ones nearest Him, tousled the hair of a couple of the oldest boys, put His hands on the backs and shoulders of the rest, and smiled warmly. We can hear Him asking their names and finding out a little about each one—where they lived, how they liked school, what their favorite activity was.

Surely some of them were shouting their answers, as children do when they are excited. Jesus probably laughed with delight as He heard stories about their daily activities. Surely two or three of the children were shy, preferring to stay in the background. Instead of ignoring them, Jesus probably addressed a couple of easy comments their way to make them feel a part of the group. He probably lifted a tiny child up on His lap and said words of kindness and comfort.

The children had to have been delighted! They had heard the adults talk about this very important man. Their daily routine had been disrupted as they had been carried to the outskirts of town to join the large crowd of onlookers. And now after hours of being quiet while their parents listened to Jesus, He was talking directly to them!

After several minutes of conversation and bantering, Jesus probably took the children one by one into His arms and pronounced His blessing on them: a special proclamation of praise for their lives and a prayer of commitment that God would bring His joy and peace to them.

If I were the parent of one of these children and had seen how Jesus' tenderness captivated His young audience, I would have wanted to relate to my children and my wife and extended family with that same kindness. How about you?

SHOWING CHRIST'S KINDNESS TO OTHERS

Can you recall a moment when someone reached out to you with kindness? Perhaps a church member showed enthusiasm when you had good news to tell. Or maybe a teacher was especially kind when you were having problems during your teen years. Or perhaps a friend comforted you during a time of personal loss or tragedy.

A warm greeting brings out the best in all of us.

For the two years that I remained in Waco, Albert was my buddy. Once he knew where my house was, he would make his way there as often as three to four times a week, just to spend time with me. (Do you suppose it was a coincidence that he'd invariably show up right at suppertime?)

Several times he was allowed to spend the night with me, even though he knew when he did he would have to pay a price: I made him take a bath. During the spring and summer months we would go swimming at the students' pool, and he would stick to me like glue. I would have predicted that he'd become rowdy and outgoing, as he had been on the bus. Instead he was very shy and insecure. I was his place of refuge. Albert and I learned to love each other dearly.

Let's look at several attitudes that lead to this godly trait of kindness.

Assume That Others Need You

Codependency, the unhealthy tendency to let our moods and actions be dictated by others, has become a buzzword in pop psychology. Counselors frequently see people who are tied to the feelings of others, and we hope to teach these people to choose an inner-directed, God-focused pattern for their lives.

However, as is the case with many good ideas, the pendulum can swing too far in the other direction. In seeking to be less dependent, these people can develop a mind-set that assumes they need little input from others: *Total self-sufficiency is where it's at!* That's taking a good idea too far.

Let's affirm the truth that we need each other in many ways. God did not give each person life only to let that person find contentment all by himself or herself. We all have needs that prompt us to seek out one another for encouragement and stimulation. Every major relationship (parent, spouse, or friend) is a conduit for the love of God.

In those college years I learned that Albert needed me in a desperate way. He had known precious little love his entire life. One Friday evening about 6:30 I was preparing for a date when my phone rang. It was Albert, and I knew immediately something was wrong because he rarely called me, even though I had given him my phone number. Since he had no phone in his house he had run several blocks to a roadside motel and called from there.

"Let, I'm scared," he said. (With his Spanish accent my name always came out "Let" instead of "Les.") "Something bad has happened, Let. Can you come help my mother?"

"Of course," was my answer. I rushed to meet him in the front yard of his ramshackle house. For the first time, I went inside and was struck immediately by the awful smell of musty furniture and spoiled food. His mother was crying, and through her broken English I deciphered that her oldest son, who was eighteen, had gotten into a nasty fight right there inside the house with some man, maybe one of her boyfriends. The man had picked up the son and thrown him so hard into the closed bedroom door, it had split in two. The man had left and the son had run to a neighbor's house.

The mother looked pitiable as she said, "You can help Albert?"

Albert stood there, looking like a whipped puppy. He needed a friend.

Sitting on the vinyl couch I looked Albert in the eyes and asked, "Albert, is there something I can do for you to make you feel less scared?"

His head hung low as he shrugged his shoulders slowly.

"Would you like to come with me for some supper, and maybe tomorrow I can take you to my house for the afternoon?"

His eyes lit up as he nodded at me then looked expectantly toward his mother, who nodded her approval. This boy hungered for affection, and I was the one who was able to give it. What an honor! What a responsibility!

When Jesus blessed the children, His message had a powerful impact on them, not just because of what He said but because of the importance of His role. As a Christian, you have several roles in which you are a unique ambassador for Christ. Have you contemplated how dearly others need you in your role as a parent, spouse, co-worker, or friend? In its own way, each role can show others a type of godly love. Never think of yourself as unnecessary. Someone needs you.

Once Albert got away with me that night he asked many questions. "Why are people mean to each other? Do you ever fight with the men you know? My mother was yelling the whole time—what was I supposed to do?" It dawned on me that my role had become one of a guide. Albert needed me; he wanted to believe there was a better way of life. He was learning to trust, and because I had been kind toward him, he was hoping I would have different answers. When Albert first caught my attention on the school bus, I could not know I would become the one to teach him about relationships and emotions. Kindness has a way of drawing people toward you.

Others need us . . . and they often need our touch.

See the Value of Touch

I have wondered what the disciples thought as they watched Jesus embrace the children. They must have felt convicted as they noticed Jesus' kindness and remembered how they had tried to push those little ones away. Perhaps they recognized how unguarded He was. How readily He laughed. How easily He handled the children's questions and comments. It didn't even seem to faze Jesus when the kids clung to His leg or clamored to sit next to Him or held up their arms to be hugged. Jesus loved the touch of children.

What is it about human touch that so powerfully creates a mood of kindness? To begin with, people read most about our feelings through nonverbal expressions. I can tell you that I support your efforts in a current project, but if my voice is bland and I stand stiffly as I speak, you probably will not believe me. However, if my voice is animated and I place my hand on your shoulder as I speak, you will feel my support. Physical contact can imply a willingness to step into another person's life. Touch conveys attachment and even commitment. Albert taught me this in a special way.

One Saturday my little buddy was helping me wash my laundry. The laundromat was only a block away from my house, so we just carried the dirty clothes in a plastic basket and walked the short distance. This particular day he was annoying me because he kept pulling on the basket I had to carry with both hands.

"Albert, you're tugging so much on my arm, I'm having a hard time carrying my load. Ease up, will you?"

"But I'm not doing anything wrong, Let." Now, normally when Albert denied wrongdoing he knew that I knew he was trying to pull one over on me. But this time he was speaking in a genuine tone of voice. Then it dawned on me. Albert wasn't pulling on my basket or trying to make me feel annoyed. He was doing the next best thing to holding hands! He wanted to touch me, to be reassured that I was right there with him.

Then I began thinking, *He does this often.* When we'd be watching a ball game on television he would sidle right up next to me. Or, after that November afternoon when I bought him the black jacket, he would be angry if he couldn't get *the* seat right behind me on the bus. He was hungry for the warmth of my touch because it told him I was as close as an arm's length. I was available.

Can you touch others naturally? When you do, are you aware of the assurance it gives you? Do you notice how it causes you to speak more kindly? And how close you feel to the other person?

Albert especially needed my touch when he met one of my college friends or when he was parading me in front of one of his school-yard buddies. Then he would touch me more than usual as if to say, "This guy belongs to me, and I belong to him. We're connected!"

I became very aware of the power my hands had to communicate all the gifts of the Christian Spirit: kindness, forgiveness, happiness, contentment—all cornerstone elements of Christian living.

In many of Jesus' healings He would lay His hands on the recipient of the miracle, not because the healing required it, but because He knew the value of His touch.

Others need us. They need our touch, and they need us to look for what is right in them.

Look for What Is Right

On that day of Jesus' interaction with the kids, we can easily assume they were behaving—well, like children. Prior to this time they might have been squirming and fretting. Perhaps some had cried and begged to be taken home. Others had complained of the heat. Some had wandered mindlessly away from their mothers. When Jesus learned of their eagerness to meet Him He could have easily replied, "Look, these kids are going to be more of a nuisance than it's worth. Tell them I said hello, but bring them back to one of My lectures when they're older." That's certainly what the disciples were thinking.

Instead, Jesus saw through their childhood imperfections. He saw children who would respond with confidence to His words of affirmation. He saw boys and girls who would delight in talking about their pets or toys. Rather than letting them be bogged down by the wrongs in their lives, He saw what was right in them.

You probably know someone who can find the good in almost any person. This quality is not phoniness or a denial of the other person's weakness, as some might assume, but a genuine desire to put people at ease.

Perhaps you know a sweet old man at church who can always remember something from your last conversation, and he readily draws attention to your accomplishments in that area. Or you may have a favorite relative who instantly puts you at ease because she overlooks your defects and praises you with genuine compliments, especially when it seems that others may be giving up on you.

Do you aspire to be that kind of person? There are several adjustments you can make to that end:

- Are you inclined to laugh sarcastically at others' problems, or do you laugh with joy at their simple pleasures?
- Check your comfort level with people who disclose personal problems. Do you try to move as quickly as possible to a safer subject, or do you express interest as you elicit more sharing?
- Be aware of your compliment-to-complaint ratio. Can you state at least five good things about others before you air your gripes?

People who are kind carefully examine their priorities because they know God's purpose for their lives is to be loving just as He is.

A powerful moment in my relationship with Albert came one Saturday when we were sitting side by side on the front steps of my rented house. It was a perfect autumn day a year after Albert and I had become friends. He was not yet ten, and I was a ripe old twenty-one. Albert was not the philosophical type, and he didn't always know what to say when I would talk with him about the Lord. But I decided I wanted him to have some understanding of God, so from time to time I'd bring up the subject.

That day the beauty of the weather seemed an appropriate segue. "Albert, you see how pretty the sky is today?"

He nodded.

"Heaven is somewhere in that direction, and God has a place saved for you if you'd like to join Him there one day." As I looked down at him—his black hair was in a curly mess as always, and he didn't look clean—I was caught by his innocence. Despite his appearance, he was a first-class kid, in my opinion. So I asked softly, "Do you think you'd like to live with God after you die?"

Looking up, Albert cocked his head and said directly to me, "Let, is God anything like you? . . . 'Cause if He is I want to go to heaven."

For a moment, I was so close to tears I couldn't talk. I put my arm around Albert as I said, "Buddy, if you think I'm nice to you, then you can multiply it by a hundred and that's how nice God is. He'll love you more than I ever could."

What was Albert thinking? Here he was, the trouble-maker who had driven every teacher, every authority figure, stark raving mad. And here I was, the idealistic psychology major who was still trying to figure out what I believed and where I was going. *Like God? Me?*

Albert knew one thing about me that mattered. I saw the good in him when precious few could. Okay, so he didn't make good grades. And maybe he was too temperamental when told no. And sometimes he acted unappreciative when something good was given to him. But he still deserved to be loved.

He was as funny as he could be. (I still laugh when I think about the way he'd run to answer my phone when it rang. He'd try to talk like me and would swear that this was "Let" speaking. I guess no one believed him, though, because they knew I didn't call myself Let.)

He was giving. Once he proudly gave me a broom that his older brother had brought home from his factory job. (No, I didn't ask if it was paid for!)

A kid who initially didn't have much to offer, Albert still had plenty of good in him, I believed. Maybe I had to look a little harder for it sometimes, but it was there!

As you consider your many relationships, can you picture how you might relate differently if you looked for what is right in other people? Could you tell a co-worker what you admire about his or her work habits more frequently? Could you be more free in expressing admiration to a friend who is always there for you? Could you thank your family more frequently for the little things they do to help around the house?

When you choose to look for what is right, your disposition naturally becomes more kind and optimistic.

Kindness means we recognize that others need us. They need our touch, they need us to look for what is right in them, and they need us to be patient.

Commit Yourself to Patience

It is hard to express kindness when you are in a hurry. Had Jesus taken about sixty seconds to step over to the children as He was leaving with His disciples, this incident would have never made an impression on anyone—neither the children nor the disciples. Certainly it would never have been included in the Gospels. His interchange with them probably lasted thirty minutes or more, much to the frustration of His disciples. Apparently He reasoned, *While I do need to get away from here, I'm not so hurried I can't take a few moments out for these kids.*

When are you in too much of a hurry to express tenderness? Are you so rushed each morning that your mood is cranky or intolerant as everyone prepares for the day's activities? Do you eat lunch too quickly to take a couple of minutes to touch base with those you work with? At church are you so pressed to leave after the service, you can't take time out for conversation?

Albert taught me patience, particularly in the early part of our relationship when he was capable of some major temper tantrums. Usually those tantrums came when I told him it was time to go home or if I told him no—like the many times he wanted to use my phone for prank calls.

One week I'd had it with Albert. He had shown up at the front door just at 6:00 P.M., so I let him come in and finish the leftovers from the supper my roommates and I had just eaten. Then I told him, "Tonight I can't do anything with you because I have to study." I motioned toward the door as I said, "Come on, I'll take you home in my car so you won't have to walk."

He didn't think much of my suggestion, but after some major grumbling I got him home. The next several days on the bus he avoided me. I spoke to him, but the look on his face and the tone of his voice told me he didn't take well to being told to go home. For a while my thoughts went something like, *Hey, if you can't accept something like a simple no, we're not going to have much of a relationship.*

But I finally reminded myself, *This boy has had nothing*

but rejection, and now he's protecting himself because he's afraid that's where we're headed. I've got to hang in there with him.

About a week later, he appeared at my front door. "Hey, Let, whachadoin?"

I asked if he had been angry at me, reminding him that he had not had much to say for several days. He shrugged and said, "Wanna watch TV?" It was his way of saying, *Let's drop it. At least you tried to be nice to me while I was in a bad mood, so I guess that counts for something.*

Several steps can help you become kinder in your relationships:

- Let conversations run their full course. Don't be too quick to cut someone off as he or she talks.

- Trim your schedule. Having a few less assignments can allow you time to be more kind and friendly.

- Watch less television. Don't allow your family schedule to revolve around the tube.

- Take time each day to do a favor that will make someone else's day go more smoothly.

I have never had a friend who could compare to Albert. I'm in my forties now with kids of my own, so I have had plenty of experiences requiring a gentle touch or a soft answer or a sincere, "I'm sorry." But Albert was my first, real, hands-on experience with someone who really, and I mean really, needed someone to say, "I'm here for you."

When we interact with others, we communicate with more than our spoken words. As we speak, others are listening with an inner ear that deciphers how sincere we are or how confident or caring or sensitive we are. People will respond to us even more when they trust our intentions than when we are overpowering.

It would have been easy for me to overlook Albert on that cold November day, and I could have gone about my business fully satisfied that I was a good guy pursuing a good life. I suppose it would have been just as easy for Jesus to have gone along with His disciples, saying, "You're right, fellows, I don't need the aggravation of having to haggle with those kids."

But I shudder to think how much I would have missed, and how much Albert would have missed, had I just gone on with my life, business as usual. Through this unlikely friendship at the very onset of my professional training, God gave me a wonderful opportunity to establish an influence in the life of someone who needed it desperately. Patience was required, and persistence was necessary. But that was a small price to pay for the lessons I learned.

OTHERS' RESPONSE TO KINDNESS

Mark's Gospel does not tell us what happened to the children after their time with Jesus. Yet it is easy to assume they (and their parents) were deeply moved that He would take the time to talk to ones so easily overlooked. We can speculate that many later became believers in His message of salvation, not *just* because they agreed with His theology, but because they could recall firsthand His kind personality, which was fully consistent with His words of God's redeeming grace.

The highlight of my relationship with Albert came one Sunday evening. I had arranged for him to be taken to a nearby church each week by a bus ministry that made runs through his neighborhood. That Saturday he was so excited he was about to burst. "Let, you have to come to my church tomorrow. I'm getting baptized, and I want you to see it."

A team of mules couldn't have pulled me away from that church the next day. When Albert stepped into the baptistery, he looked into the small audience to see if I had come. He tried to maintain a reverent facade, but when he spotted me, his face broke into a huge grin.

He didn't have a deep knowledge of Jesus, but I had told him all a boy his age and ability could manage. And I'm sure the angels sang when he professed that he had accepted Jesus as his Savior. Now he was in the kind hands of God.

His Confidence:

The Confrontation with Pilate

John 18

Have you ever been called to testify in court? It's a nerve-racking experience you never forget. I have been called numerous times to testify as an expert witness about a person's emotional fitness. Through experience, I've learned a few of the ins and outs of the legal game, but I will never be comfortable in this role.

When I'm on the witness stand, one attorney is trying to make me look as brilliant as Einstein himself while the other is painting me as a hick who just fell off the turnip truck. My reputation is at stake, as is the future of the person I am testifying about, so I become quite apprehensive. It takes a lot of confidence just to survive such an ordeal.

Yet each day we live we are giving witness to those who would put our character on trial. When we know our character is being evaluated, how do we respond? Are we angry? Defensive? Insecure? Apologetic? Do we turn into people pleasers? Actors? Tap dancers? Whether we are being sized up by people who know us intimately or by casual acquaintances, we need to show confidence in our character.

Let's take a hard look at the requirements for confidence by examining a page from the life of Christ just prior to His execution. Recall that from the moment Jesus began His public ministry He was under intense scrutiny, more than you and I could ever imagine. The Pharisees and other leaders in His culture did all they could to keep folks in line by insisting on conformity. You know the stories of how Jesus eluded the many traps laid for Him until the final Passover Week, when He was arrested and put through the humiliation of a mock trial. Once the Jewish leaders had Him safely under wraps, they were determined to eliminate His influence permanently. Throughout this process, Jesus displayed an inner strength, a confidence, that inspires us still today.

Late at night, while Jesus and His disciples were in the garden of Gethsemane, they were startled by the forceful sounds of the approaching Roman soldiers. Accompanied by temple officials, the soldiers made their way through the olive trees, carrying bright torches that lit up the night. They arrested Jesus and took Him first to the house of Annas and then to Caiaphas and the Sanhedrin to be ridiculed by the ruling elite. Formal legal proceedings were suspended as phony witnesses testified against Him. The night wore on as the testimony became increasingly intense. But through it all, Jesus remained silent, even when asked to speak in His own defense.

Because the rulers were in such a riotous mood, little provocation was required to beat Jesus unmercifully. He was blindfolded, then spat upon, then struck repeatedly in the face. Grown men, presumably well respected in the community, were reduced to barbarism because of their hatred for Him. Their pitiable behavior was a thin disguise for their enormous insecurity. All the while, Jesus declined to say anything on His own behalf, absorbing whatever blows and insults they hurled at Him.

You can probably recall no time in your own life when you were so shamefully mistreated. Yet you may recall times when you felt vulnerable to personal attack. Perhaps you are all too aware that legalistically minded people will reject you once they learn of your flaws or frailties, so you try hard to keep them covered. Maybe you have been the recipient of past sexual or physical abuse that has left inner scars that make you doubt your worthiness. Perhaps you have been through a divorce or you are having major marital problems but you dare not expose your needs because you fear what people will think. Like Jesus, we each have our own potential tormentors who would rob us of our dignity or security.

When I am testifying in a courtroom and come under severe attack, I cannot help but waver inwardly, no matter how strong I attempt to appear outwardly. I begin to question the wisdom of my decisions and wonder about my value as a person. I defensively want to explain myself out of any holes the attorneys might create for me. I do not naturally respond as Jesus did, resolute and unbaffled.

As daybreak neared after Jesus' all-night trial, He was taken to the place of the visiting Roman governor, Pontius Pilate. Called the Praetorium, the complex probably included Pilate's residence, some military barracks, and a judgment chamber for dealing with legal disputes. In their pious hypocrisy, the Jewish leaders would not permit themselves to enter a Gentile's domain, so they presented their case to Pilate outdoors. Pilate wanted nothing to do with this problem once he heard their weak evidence that Jesus was an insurrectionist. Yet because he was a politician he chose to humor the Jews by detaining Jesus for private questioning.

It was inside the Praetorium that Jesus' confidence was most clearly on display. Unaware that he was speaking to the Son of Almighty God, Pilate began his questioning with condescension. Half annoyed and half amused, he asked, "Are You the King of the Jews?"

Knowing Pilate had no jurisdiction over Him except what was allowed by God, Jesus responded, "Are you speaking for yourself about this, or did others tell you this concerning Me?" (John 18:34).

Through this response, Jesus calmly implied, *Sir, I am in no way threatened by you or your potential pronouncements.*

If you want to talk with Me, let's start by avoiding games and being straight with each other. At this moment, a defining point came in the interchange between Pilate and Jesus. No longer was Jesus' character the one on trial; instead, Pilate now felt compelled to defend his position.

Angrily Pilate snapped that he cared nothing about the Jews' internal affairs. "Am I a Jew? Your own . . . chief priests have delivered You to me. What have You done?" (John 18:35).

Again, Jesus spoke with firm but calm assurance. "My kingdom is not of this world. If My kingdom were of this world, My servants would fight, so that I should not be delivered to the Jews; but now My kingdom is not from here" (John 18:36). Jesus was refusing to explain the actions of others. The point was, He knew who He was and why He was in this position, so He refrained from being involved in Pilate's circular arguments. This bothered Pilate, but he was too proud to admit his crumbling sense of adequacy. What a contrast between a self-assured character and one riddled by phoniness!

Which one of these men are we most like? When under attack by others do we know who we are so that we do not get caught in unnecessary defensiveness? Or do we quickly go down to the level of the one rejecting us, choosing to engage in a fruitless game of one-upmanship? It's all too easy to fall into such a trap!

With a false show of machismo, Pilate probed, "Are You a king then?"

Imagine Pilate's discomfort when Jesus openly affirmed his statement, saying, in essence, "That's right. I *am* a king. This is why I was born, and My royal mission is to bear witness of truth. If you were a seeker of truth you would hear Me" (see John 18:37).

By this time, Pilate was weakening. I can hear him mumbling, "What is truth?"

Jesus was unwavering in the face of derisive questioning and Roman authority. His confidence was so ingrained it was an impenetrable armor. No other person spoke on His behalf. He simply clung to His identity as God's representative and would not allow Pilate to shake Him from His mission.

BUILDING A CONFIDENCE ANCHORED IN GOD'S STRENGTH

Being less defensive and more confident requires us to take the time, when life is calm, to ponder who we are (as Jesus did many times). Then, as we learn to anticipate our responses in vulnerable circumstances, we will be more likely to wear an armor of confidence that comes from knowing our secure position in God.

Confidence is one of the traits that attracts a lot of attention in counseling. One person who made major adjustments in this realm was Becky, a twenty-nine-year-old single mother who originally sought counseling for anxiety attacks. She had recently been divorced and admitted that she had contributed to the marital tension by being worrisome and easily frustrated. Now on her own with a six-year-old daughter, Becky had many fears about her new life and how she could best provide for her daughter's future.

Becky had an engaging personality, and she spoke freely as we talked. She said, "I wish my bad moods wouldn't come over me so quickly. It seems like one minute I'm just fine, then something can set me off and I can't shake my dark feelings."

"Can you give me an example?"

"Yes. Last night I ate dinner with my parents. They keep Jennifer for me after school. During our table talk, my dad just casually questioned why I had been buying Jennifer so many new clothes. He can be pretty critical, and I knew he was about to jump on my case. I *hadn't* been buying anything unusual for my daughter, so I quickly became defensive. He didn't press the issue, but for the rest of the evening I was upset because I get so tired of being quizzed whenever I'm around my parents. It's like they don't trust me."

"Becky, how far back does this tension go?"

"For as long as I can remember. I was real friendly in my school days, but I guess you could say I was constantly looking over my shoulder, wondering what people thought about me. I was the same way in my married years, too worried about what people thought and constantly tied in knots because of it. My husband never could understand why it was so important to me to keep other people happy, and maybe he had a good point. Maybe I'm too much of a people pleaser."

As Becky talked, she revealed several things that explained her lack of confidence: A critical dad. A peace-at-all-costs mother. An emphasis on external beauty. Her attempts to keep up with the popular crowd. Winning approval through achievements. Protesting too strongly if someone challenged her. Arguing at the drop of a hat. These signs and more told me she needed to become anchored in a belief in herself that transcended human opinions.

In our sessions we concentrated on several insights that could lead her toward a Christ-centered confidence. At first Becky was uncertain she could change. After all, she was working against a strong history of self-doubt. But I explained to her that while change would not come overnight it could happen if she applied new concepts to many of her daily circumstances. It's never too late for any of us to rethink who we are.

Together we talked about some tried-and-true adjustments that could help her live with a faith in herself that was anchored in God's strength.

Learn to Read the Meaning of Your Behavior

Think of situations when you need to stand firmly against potential opposition—major trials or just everyday occurrences. Consider what your behavior says about your level of confidence. For example, your child does not like the request you have made, so he becomes defiant. Are you defensive or even-keeled? Your impatience with your kids can imply a lack of confidence in your ability to communicate with them in a way that will lead to family harmony.

Or, as you confront your spouse with a frustration, it becomes clear he or she disagrees with your perceptions.

At that point do you retreat? Repeat yourself many times? If you withdraw in silence you may imply that you feel incapable of showing your feelings successfully. If you repeat yourself in a heated argument it shows that you feel uncertain you will be taken seriously.

Or you may focus on how different you are from the other adults in your extended family. When you are with them, how do you act? Are you constantly fretting about your looks or worrying about something else? Are you as compliant as ever? Do you struggle to control your irritation over seemingly minor things? If you fret about the way you look or about how well you communicate, it illustrates a discomfort in letting people see your real humanness. When you worry, it shows how uncertain you are regarding your own decision-making skills. When you are persistently grouchy, you are assuming that others do not care about you . . . and it is causing you to doubt whether you have any influence.

Many circumstances, large or small, illustrate our levels of confidence. In fact, the best way to determine whether you have this trait is to examine your emotional outlook. If you struggle too often with impatience or defensiveness or guilt or worry, you are probably insecure. As you become increasingly aware of these feelings, consider how you might handle yourself differently in situations where they are likely to occur. Could you use fewer words to explain yourself? Could you be freer and more open? Could you allow others to think what they wanted, even if they were wrong?

Becky once told me, "I guess I never realized how often

I show myself to be insecure. But if insecurity is demonstrated through each of my negative traits, I've really got my work cut out!"

"Don't be discouraged," I assured her. "By knowing how your lack of confidence plays out in your lifestyle, you can focus on reversing that weakness. As you find yourself pleading your case too strongly, recognize that your communication at that moment is propelled by insecurity. When you recognize what's happening, ask yourself, *Is this the attitude I truly want right now?* You *need* that awareness so you can begin the process of challenging your guiding thoughts."

"I like the way you explain that," she replied, "because it allows me to be honest about my negative traits without being self-condemning."

Over time, you can get caught in habits (anger, defensiveness, withdrawal) that are subconsciously pushed along by your lack of confidence. Once you become aware that your behaviors reflect an underlying insecurity, you can make the necessary adjustments.

To develop the confidence you need, begin by rethinking where your worth comes from. Is it given to you by humans or is your worth an undeniable truth that is established solely by God?

Remember, Worth Comes from God Alone

Not too long ago a former secretary of mine brought her brand-new baby to our offices. Can you guess my reaction to the little child? I smiled at her, bent over and said a few silly remarks about how cute she was. I congratulated her proud mom and told her I wished nothing but the best for them both. Why this response? I was operating on a very basic assumption that this child was a gift from God who deserved to be properly loved. No one had to tell me that she was valuable; I held this belief by instinct. Deep within our hearts we know that each human individual is a valuable treasure.

Now, shift gears and suppose your family did not communicate clearly to you in your early years a sense of your basic worth. Perhaps they took good care of your physical needs (clothing you, feeding you, sending you off to school or sports) but failed to reinforce your value. Does that mean your worth ceases to exist? No, it only means it was not properly taught to you. You probably struggle with a deep-seated insecurity; you may hear from spiritually minded people that you are valuable before God, yet your experiences with humans prove otherwise. What are you to do?

That was Becky's problem. She told me, "I don't doubt that my mother and father loved me, yet when I was growing up they had some odd ways of treating me." She went on to explain that she rarely felt she could please her parents, who seemed to constantly criticize her for typical childhood flaws. She believed the restrictions they put on her were not always reasonable. Accusations were made. "It was like they gave lip service to my worth, but their behaviors reflected an attitude of rejection."

"When experiences like that stand out in your memory," I said, "you will naturally wonder if you really do have any value as a person. We can add to that the major rejection that comes with a divorce. The result is a lack of confidence that's evidenced in your worry and depression. You need to be convinced that God has never given up on you. He deemed you lovable on the day you were born, and His opinion has not changed since."

She quickly interjected, "I've heard many times that God loves me, but it all seems so theoretical. How can I make this concept more real?"

"Let's use a little logic here," I said, with a twinkle in my eye. "If you, in fact, were a worthless person and you knew it through and through, would you ever experience troublesome emotions like discouragement or tension or frustration?"

Cocking her head to one side, she thought briefly then smiled. "I suppose not. If I thought I was truly worthless I just wouldn't care."

"Likewise, if you were a truly worthless person and you knew it through and through, would you ever feel *positive* emotions in the wake of something good, emotions like happiness or contentment or excitement?"

Once again she smiled. "Not really, because if I had no worth I'd have no reason to be glad that something good happened to me."

"You have what we might call a 'worth mechanism' within your personality that knows when others have or have not recognized its existence," I said, pausing as she nodded to let me know she was following my reasoning. Then I asked her, "Can you tell me where you got this mechanism?"

"I can't really say I got it from anyone or anyplace, except to say that it's been in me all my life."

And that was my point. The matter of individual worth is not just a nice-sounding theory based on someone's desire to give you warm, feel-good messages. It is an unwavering fact established by God and explained in Scripture. When a person treats us unworthily, we need to remind ourselves that this person does not have the ultimate authority of God. We desire positive treatment from others, but when we receive unfavorable treatment instead, we can remain steady, knowing our worth was given to us from God and it cannot be taken away by some thoughtless remark or action.

Jesus was severely mistreated by persons who had no conception of His innate worth before God. What is worse, some of His tormenters actually claimed to be God's representatives. But instead of feeling inadequate in the face of such derision, Jesus remained focused on who He was to God. This did not necessarily take away His feelings of disappointment and torment, but it gave Him unshakable confidence. And this confidence helped Him keep His defensiveness to a minimum.

Minimally Defend Yourself

As I read and reread the accounts of Jesus' rejection by the church and the civic leaders, I am amazed by His lack of strong self-defense. Even when He did respond to Pilate's questions, He did not elaborate or express shock that His words were so summarily overlooked.

When I am feeling persecuted or rejected, my first inclination is to defend myself. I can barely tolerate the thought that someone would pronounce judgment on me without knowing all the facts. So I often feel compelled to fill in the missing pieces. Rarely does it work! But I do it anyway.

Think of some common moments when you slip into patterns of unnecessary self-defense: Perhaps a fellow employee complains that his productivity is being hindered because of your work pace, and you protest that you have endured great difficulty in trying to get the project done. Or maybe a family member frowns as she watches you discipline one of your children, and you immediately feel you must explain how the child has been defying your authority for the past several days. Or you might spill some food on the front of your clothes when you are away from home and then, without being asked, explain to several people throughout the day what happened.

Is it wrong to defend your feelings or behaviors? Not necessarily. Sometimes you genuinely need to clarify your actions to others, but it *is* possible to defend yourself so frequently or so unnecessarily that you put your insecurities on open display.

To display confidence, you will probably benefit by scaling down your defenses. Explain yourself only when another person is confused; use explanations, not to defuse judgments but to provide enlightenment. (You will know the difference based on the amount of pleading and persuasion you use.) Once you have made the necessary clarifying statements, don't repeat yourself.

When Becky and I discussed this concept, she shook her head. "Dr. Carter, I seem to defend myself every day. And when I'm not openly making self-protective statements, I'm inwardly thinking them. It would feel very odd to drop this tendency. I guess I'm wanting more control over people's thoughts about me."

"I'm operating on the assumption that the more you work to make yourself look acceptable, the less likely people will actually accept you," I explained. "Whether or not they are aware of it, they are looking to you for signals to tell them what they should think about you. When they hear you constantly backpedaling to cover your tracks, they naturally wonder what is so wrong in you that requires such an ongoing defense.

"Conversely, when you speak calmly, you send the signal that you think well of yourself. People will pick up on that and will, more likely than not, respect who you are."

When Becky's dad criticized her decisions, she told him she would consider his input, but she refrained from trying to convince him she really was not as wrong as he thought. She let her calm demeanor speak for itself. When her ex-husband said something unflattering about her, she remembered that he was not very objective about her, and she did not feel compelled to correct him.

By dropping your defenses, you show that you have no desire to manipulate another's thoughts—nor will you be manipulated by him or her. You will be committed to a mind-set that says, *Let's take each other where we are.*

When Jesus stood before Pilate, He knew who He was in God. He was confident that He had nothing to hide nor any reason to sell Himself to any man because He knew

God was with Him. Likewise, He was aware that if Pilate was, in fact, a seeker of truth, He would weigh the evidence about Him and see what was right; if not, no amount of pleading or persuasion would matter.

Realize the Insecurity Behind Others' Judgments

Christ was a master at understanding the person behind the public mask. In Pilate He saw a man who overtly exuded power but was only a cynical, emotionally cautious man. (These traits were publicly displayed as he appealed to the crowd to determine Jesus' fate, rather than standing on the strength of his governmental position.) Rather than arguing with Pilate, Jesus chose to speak confidently in the knowledge that Pilate was just as human as anyone else who had questioned Him. Knowing who Pilate really was also helped Jesus remember who He was.

Can you size people up accurately enough to know when to sidestep their "invitations" to get caught in their games? If others are too accusing or judgmental, there is a war going on inside them . . . a war you are not required to participate in. These insecure people usually do not admit their insecurities; instead they find ways to stroke their own egos by putting others down.

When I talked with Becky about this concept, she agreed with me in theory, but she also admitted that she had difficulty applying this insight. "It would almost seem blasphemous to believe that someone as important as my dad is insecure. All my life I've held my parents in awesome regard, to the extent that they've had a godlike hold on me."

"Understand that I have no desire for you to lose your respect for them," I assured her. "But I *am* suggesting that it's time that you see all adults, including your parents, for what they are. Each of us is imperfect. Each of us has insecurities. We have all failed. Therefore, none of us has a right to devalue anyone else."

"If I look at my parents as fellow humans who have behind-the-scenes struggles with self-esteem just as I do, it would make a major difference in the way I feel about myself."

"That's right!" I said. "Don't make the mistake of assuming that everyone but you has his or her act together."

Paradoxically, secure people show their stability when they can admit how insecure they sometimes feel. In the same way, insecure people show their instability by having to be above others. When you sense that you are being pulled into a game of one-upmanship, as Pilate was doing to Jesus, you can make a conscious decision to sidestep whatever statements are made to undermine your confidence.

Several specific adjustments will occur as you increase your inner confidence:

- You will cease to apologize for actions that are not wrong or harmful.
- You can state your feelings or ideas without unnecessary justification.

- If others choose to think poorly of you in spite of your best efforts to do what is right, you will acknowledge that they have this prerogative.
- You can smile at your own slipups.
- You will be proper in social etiquette, but you will not go overboard to impress.

Being confident means that no matter what opinions others hold of you, you will choose to be God-directed in your life.

MAINTAINING CONFIDENCE REGARDLESS OF THE RESPONSE

When you are genuinely confident, you are likely to encounter varying reactions. One reaction may be admiration. Some people genuinely admire and are attracted to those who are secure and confident in themselves. People who react this way feed positively from the strength our confidence exudes.

Others, however, may react negatively because they may view our confidence as a threat to their need for power. They may reject us as a way to hide their own inadequacies. This was what happened when Jesus was brought before Pilate. In the end, Pilate collapsed under the pressure to put Jesus to death, meaning he must have also maintained some animosity toward Him.

Regardless of how others respond to your growing confidence, resolve to let the Holy Spirit guide you rather than handing over your confidence to inconsistent humans. Remember Jesus' example and strive to develop a confidence that's anchored in God's strength and built upon your identity as one of His cherished children.

His Objectivity:

The Woman at the Well

John 4:3–42

Whendi was seven years old, my dad took a chaplain's position at a home for unwed mothers. At that time, if an unmarried woman became pregnant she would likely be sent away in secret to hide the shame of her behavior.

"The home," as we called it, was a place of waiting for the arrival of the baby, who probably would be earmarked for adoption. Even if they were as old as forty, the residents were called "the girls" and would participate in classes or work at part-time jobs while they lived in the dormitory. There they received nutritional guidance and spiritual and psychological counseling to ease them through this difficult time.

Dad was not shy about exposing me to his work. My brother, sister, and I were frequent visitors to the home for unwed mothers, and we enjoyed hanging out at the recreation hall, waiting to see who might come along and give us a little extra attention. Every Friday Dad would obtain a film from a local TV station, and we would have an "evening at the movies" with the girls, there in the wide-open rec room.

I looked forward to those Fridays. Since most residents would stay five months or longer, I would get to know many of them by name. Somehow, I would manage a cozy position each week between two of my favorites on the oversized couch. It didn't matter what movie was playing. I was content, knowing I'd get the same cute compliments week after week from the ladies I grew to love.

I remember my excitement one day when Dad asked me, "Do you remember a lady named Judy who lived here about a year ago?"

Of course I did. She had taken a special liking to me and had always sought me out for a bear hug. She was one of my all-time favorites.

"Well, Judy is coming back for another stay. You will be seeing her again real soon."

That was terrific news! My pal was coming back for another five-month stint! This meant more hugs, and I knew I could always talk her into getting me a candy bar from the machine. I couldn't wait until the first Friday after her arrival.

You see, at that age I was too naive to know I was supposed to look down on people like Judy. She had committed a mortal sin, not once but twice, and her family sent her to us because they knew of no other way to handle their embarrassment. But none of that mattered to me. I simply knew that she was real nice, and my dad told me she wanted to understand how God could be real in her life. That made good sense to me. In a way, I wish I were still that naive.

JESUS' FAIRNESS AND OBJECTIVITY

Jesus was not naive, but He refused to be bound by society's preferences and attitudes. Being God's emissary, He chose to maintain fairness in His dealings with people, even those who were very different from Him. He displayed objectivity.

An illustration of His objectivity is recorded in John 4, the familiar story of the woman at the well.

Jesus and His disciples had spent an extensive period of time in Jerusalem and the surrounding regions of southern Israel. They were tired and ready to head northward to their Galilean home so, instead of bypassing Samaria, as most Jews did, Jesus chose to cut straight through. The disciples probably griped about this, but that did not deter the Master.

They stopped at the outskirts of the town called Sychar late one afternoon. Jesus sent the twelve disciples into town for supplies as He lingered by an old well. He was worn out.

Soon, a local woman approached the well, and Jesus knew instantly that she had a troubled past. She was probably middle-aged, and her worn, haggard look spoke of years of wanton living.

True to His friendly nature, Jesus engaged her in conversation by asking her for a drink of water. The woman was not sure how to respond. Women in her day were not held in high esteem by men who didn't associate with them in public. So why was this man talking to her? And she immediately recognized that He was an outsider, a Jew who would normally ignore such a hated Samaritan.

The enmity between the Samaritans and Jews had begun centuries earlier. The early Jewish kings, David and Solomon, had built a strong political coalition with the inhabitants of Canaan, so during their reigns peace was relatively constant. But after Solomon died, Israel was increasingly vulnerable to the outside influences of pagans, particularly the Syrians and Assyrians (from what is now modern Iraq).

The middle section of Israel, known in Jesus' time as Samaria, was particularly vulnerable to this outside influence. The terrain there was such that the people could not readily defend themselves from invaders, so outsiders (particularly the Assyrians) settled there, plundered the land, intermarried with the Jews, and imposed their religion upon the people. By Jesus' day, the people of Samaria were different from those who lived in the northern and southern sections of Israel. Idol worship had become common, and people ignored Mosaic law.

The Samaritans were known as traitors and sellouts, and they were hated by the devout Jews. This fierce enmity toward Samaritans was the reason Jews traveling between northern and southern Israel took the longer route around Samaria; they wanted to avoid contact with these outcasts.

If you follow world news today, you know that many Middle Easterners still have difficulty being objective with one another because their emotions run so high. This caused just as many problems in Jesus' day as it does now.

All this was the unspoken backdrop behind Jesus' strange encounter with the Samaritan woman at the well. Startled by Jesus' friendly gesture, the woman asked defensively, "How is it that You, being a Jew, ask a drink from me, a Samaritan woman?" (John 4:9).

Jesus' reply was cryptic. He hinted that she should realize He was a special person sent from the Lord who could do a lot more for her. He could give her living water.

Not understanding His analogy, she pointed out an obvious problem: He did not have a bucket to fetch any water, and the well was very deep.

Jesus may have chuckled inwardly at her inability to relate to Him. How would He present His message in a way she would understand? Again He used the water analogy, saying He had a message that would give her eternal life. Still baffled, and probably annoyed, the woman replied, in essence, "Like I said, give me some of Your eternal water that I may not thirst again or have to come here twice a day to draw water."

Was she being sarcastic, or was she genuinely unsure of what He was saying? We don't know for sure, but we do know that Jesus pressed on with great patience.

Stop for a moment to consider times when you have wanted to explain something important to someone who clearly was not catching the drift of what you were saying. If you are like me, you began feeling impatient or annoyed. You may have thought, *Why can't this person hear what I'm trying to say?* Your emotions begin to rise as your objectivity wanes. Being human, Jesus had to be susceptible to these inner reactions, but He was strong enough to keep His composure and maintain a course that would be helpful to the woman.

It is at this point that Jesus introduced the subject of the woman's marital status. When she said she was not married, He leveled with her, telling her, in effect, "I know you're not currently married, but I also know you've had five previous husbands and you now have a live-in boyfriend."

I'm sure her jaw dropped as she said the first thing she could think of: "You must be some kind of prophet." A safe assumption!

Was Jesus trying to embarrass her when He introduced the subject of her checkered past? Or was He trying to gain the upper hand? Not at all. He had perceived that she was emotionally unstable, prone to many highs and lows. He wanted to clearly communicate a major point: "You are correct that I'm a prophet who has much wisdom to share. But before you think I am too pious to relate to someone like yourself, let Me inform you that your personal ups and downs don't blow Me away. Whatever you tell Me about yourself, I can handle."

Jesus held many notions about proper and improper behavior. Yet those notions were not so powerful that they "permitted" Him to look upon this woman with scorn. In spite of His clear differentness from her, He was objective and fair with her.

Each of us can surely recall many moments each day when such objectivity could be used. Consider these common scenarios:

- In a phone conversation with a family member, you sense he or she is being unnecessarily critical, and this arouses your frustration. Can you learn to separate yourself from his or her inappropriate criticism, or do you fume for a long time about this person's difficult character?

- You have been informed by a friend that another person rejects you. Do you obsess about why this rejection occurs, or can you accept the truth that you will not always be held in high regard by everybody?

Developing an Attitude of Objectivity

Objectivity is not always easy or natural. We are prone to respond to situations with our feelings, especially when our emotions sneak up on us. Often we must think through potentially vulnerable circumstances in advance so our responses can be implemented just as readily. By preparing in advance for these situations, we can develop attitudes that help us react objectively in challenging circumstances.

Let's examine four attitudes that will help us learn to react objectively in circumstances when we might be vulnerable to bias and out-of-control emotions.

I Am Not Easily Shocked

In my counseling office it is common for someone to say, "You're not going to believe what I'm about to tell you." Although I don't usually say it, I'm thinking, *Try me. I've probably heard some variation of this before.*

Very few things shock me. I suppose that could imply a hardness, but I do not intend to be that way. Rather, I have concluded that people, even good and decent people, are capable of just about anything. Jeremiah 17:9 is not flattering, but it cuts to the core of things: "The heart is deceitful above all things, / And desperately wicked; / Who can know it?" People can get involved in all sorts of negative predicaments.

Some people let their no-shock mind-set feed a cynical view of people. They hold others in low regard and conclude that people are no good or are not to be trusted. Such cynicism goes too far. When I suggest that we should not be easily shocked I only mean it is not fair to hold people to idealistic expectations; we must allow our fellow human beings to be just that—human.

That's the mind-set Jesus maintained with the woman at the well. He understood who she was, but He did not hold that against her. Go back to the scenarios I just described and see if you can apply this no-shock mind-set to each:

- In a phone conversation with a family member you sense he or she is being unnecessarily critical, but you remember this person has struggled with this problem for years. While you do not like his or her critical nature, you remain calm in the assurance that you are under no obligation to change or correct him or her.
- You have been informed by a friend that another person rejects you. Rejection is never pleasant, so it is normal to feel hurt; yet you remind yourself that this person is not God.

I suppose people most frequently expect me to be shocked when their story has something to do with a moral or ethical failure. I remember feeling frustrated after a series of seven or eight counseling sessions with a man because we did not seem to be making much headway. Finally he began one session by leaning forward in his chair and saying, "I've been debating since my first visit if I could tell you something, and I've decided today's the day." He went on to explain how he had been addicted to pornography for years and his real goal for counseling was to overcome this.

"Why did you wait so long to tell me this?" I asked.

"On one other occasion I tried to talk this out with a Christian friend, but it soon became apparent that he was blown away by it. He told me, 'My view of you is so inconsistent with what you are telling me, I just can't handle it.' Right then and there I decided I couldn't be open with people."

How would you handle it if a close friend or family member revealed something to you that was controversial or incriminating?

People *can* be rude or aloof or irresponsible or confused; this fact will not go away as long as we live on this side of heaven. When we allow our emotions to determine our responses to others' imperfections, it is usually because of our secret desire to rewrite reality. But no matter how hard we wish, truth cannot be written. It simply *is*. Our job is to determine the most spiritually and emotionally healthy response to reality. How many of the following statements do you have a hard time openly accepting?

- People can be rude or unfair to me even when I try my best to be reasonable.
- Marriage takes real work, and sometimes it can feel really futile.
- I am sometimes prone to difficult emotions like depression or insecurity or resentment.
- I may never make the kind of money that will take me to easy street.
- It may sometimes seem impossible to live with a consistent feeling of victory in my Christian walk.

These statements represent a few of the hard truths each of us faces. The more difficulty we have with them (and others like them) the more we will struggle to be objective.

But conversely, as we learn to accommodate these truths, we will find greater emotional stability.

To be objective we must keep from being easily shocked, and we must also allow people to be who they really are.

I Allow People to Be Who They Really Are

We respond to circumstances based upon the way they please or displease our desires. If you do me an unexpected favor, I respond with delight. If you fail to do what you promised, I respond with annoyance. This response pattern is very normal, yet it can also be dangerous if left unchecked.

To keep our demands from becoming extreme, we must be mindful of the inherent freedom each person possesses. God set into motion well-defined standards of right and wrong, then He stepped back and allowed us the freedom to abide by those standards we choose. We are free to make poor choices just as readily as good ones.

Yet emotionally overcharged people have difficulty with this freedom since their emotions keep bringing them back to their own desires and preferences. They lose their objectivity.

Did Jesus have opinions about divorce or adultery? Of course He did. Those beliefs are clearly spelled out elsewhere in Scripture. Then why would He seem so accommodating to the woman who had violated those opinions to the extreme? Because He recognized her freedom to be what she was.

Back in the days of Dad's work at the home for unwed

mothers, I recall his helping me to understand Judy better. "Son, do you know what it means to be depressed?" he asked me.

I never liked having to admit ignorance, but I honestly did not understand the word, and I said so.

"Well, Judy has been feeling depressed. You see, last year when she came here she made a promise to herself that she would not get pregnant until she got married, but it didn't work out that way. So she's pretty down on herself."

Dad went on to explain, as best as he could to a seven-year-old, that having babies was something people should not do unless they were married. It was outside God's design. Judy was depressed because she was frustrated with herself.

So how did I act whenever I would see Judy after learning this about her? Did I ignore her? Give her an icy glare? Frown and shake my head? Talk to her about virtuous living? I can easily picture these things happening if an adult were trying to make sense of Judy's depression. But I was a seven-year-old kid, so I responded the way any child would: I accepted her with no questions asked. I let Judy be Judy.

Isn't it amazing how young kids relate so freely? Unencumbered by strong opinions or religious correctness, it doesn't dawn on them to fit people into a box. That comes later, once they grow up and receive knowledge.

On the Friday night after that talk, I waited in the rec room for Judy. I never liked that time of waiting because I was always eager to connect with my pals. But finally she walked in, talking casually with another resident. She didn't seem depressed to me; in fact she was smiling. I stood back, not wanting to appear anxious, but she called out to me and motioned toward the couch. She had to have been at least six months pregnant by then, so I tried not to be too rough as I plopped down next to her.

We talked for a few moments about my day—how school was and all that. Then I looked up at her and said, "It's okay if you feel sad. I don't mind."

She smiled as if to say, *Where'd that come from?* Then she said, "Well, how can I be sad when I'm sitting next to a good-looking guy like you?"

That's all it took. As far as I was concerned, Judy didn't have to meet any more requirements for me. Maybe I wouldn't have been able to discuss it too deeply, but if she had wanted to talk about her feelings that would have been fine by me.

When I talk with people about allowing others to be free, I usually get some agreement. After all, it's hard to argue against the fact that God made each of us with a free will. Often, though, I hear a quick *but,* signifying that the person is not willing to fully accept another person's freedom. Consider the following statements.

- "I know my husband is free to have his own perspective on child-rearing, *but . . .*"
- "I'm aware that my kids are free to have bad moods, *but . . .*"
- "I realize others may not like the same social activities I do, *but . . .*"

It can be hard to allow others to be free because there is always the distinct possibility they will use their freedom wrongly. Don't misunderstand me. I'm not suggesting you should never assert your own opinions or ideas. I *am* suggesting, though, that you allow other people to sift out their own responses. Jesus clearly wanted the woman at the well to choose a better way of life. But rather than imposing His will on her by an impassioned plea, He allowed her to respond to Him in her own timing.

When I was a child visiting the home for unwed mothers, Judy liked being with me because I had no desire to make her fit a mold. Now, in retrospect, I wonder whether she would have experienced a lot less depression if a few adults in her life had responded to her with as much objectivity as an unaware seven-year-old boy.

To be objective we must keep from being easily shocked, we must allow people to be who they really are, and we must have our own separate game plan.

I Have My Own Separate Game Plan

Jesus' interaction with the woman at the well was not unlike many exchanges among other folks, both in Jesus' time and in ours. She was as confused and insecure as He was certain and stable. Imagine yourself in a situation when you honestly believe your ways are unquestionably better than someone else's. At that moment, will you be able to remain calm, or will you get pulled into the emotion of the moment?

Jesus was able to maintain objectivity because He was committed to a plan of life set before Him by God. Even when individuals did not support His plan or understand His ways, He still kept His focus on that plan.

I must have been eight or nine when Dad taught me to have my own game plan. He was still chaplain at the home for unwed mothers, and he was preparing a lesson for his Sunday worship service. It was near Easter, and we were going over the plans for the candlelight service. I was miffed because I was not going to do the important job of lighting the first candle. That one fell to Dad.

"I'm going to be speaking about the subject of living for Christ," Dad explained. I always felt proud when he would tell me these kinds of things because it made me feel important. "I'm going to challenge the girls to think about what it means to live as He would want them to live."

Then he looked reflectively toward me and asked, "Les, if you could describe how you think God wants you to live, what would you come up with?"

I sure didn't want to give the "I-don't-know" answer most of my buddies would have given. So I said, "Well, I guess I'd want to be kind to people, just like Jesus was."

"I like that," he said, "and I want you to concentrate on being that way, even when others in your life might not be cooperating."

I knew there had to be a catch to it; there always was. Later when my twin brother and I were not getting along well, which is a nice way of saying we were arguing incessantly, my dad reminded me of my goal to have my own game plan. Then he went on to say, "Les, when your brother is not doing the things you want him to do, your tendency is to shower him with criticism and advice he doesn't want or need. This sets you up to be disappointed when he chooses not to follow your advice."

He recognized that I was very capable of losing my objectivity, although at the time I would not have understood the word. "I wonder if you could imagine yourself giving him a different reaction the next time he chooses not to be what you want him to be."

I knew Dad would not have appreciated my real thoughts about fighting back harder, so I tried to come up with an acceptable answer. "I guess if he's in a bad mood I could leave him alone. Then we wouldn't fight."

"That's a good alternative. Would you ever want to offer him forgiveness?"

"I guess I could." I knew where Dad was going with the discussion, and I realized he was right, but I found his concept less than neutral. He wanted me to choose my own game plan for life without getting pulled off course by a rowdy or uncooperative brother.

When I ask people to describe the traits they want most in their personalities, no one ever responds with the desire to be grouchy or bossy or impatient or insecure. I help people realize they are letting someone else set their emotional agenda when these negative qualities persist. An alternative would be to contemplate some of your common tension-producing scenarios and then think of an objective game plan that you might adopt.

Jesus knew who He was, and He had contemplated God's plan for living all His life. Therefore, no event or person would be powerful enough to move Him away from His goals. While you and I cannot expect to live with this perfect consistency, we can determine to relate fairly, even in the face of another person's ups and downs.

To be objective we must keep from being easily shocked, we must allow people to be who they really are, we must have our own separate game plan, and we must allow for differences in temperament.

I Allow for Differences in Temperament

Several years ago I attended a professional seminar on a temperament analysis test that showed how individuals could be categorized into one of four general temperament styles. The instructor explained that the test had been given to five hundred executives of major corporations. Then he challenged us: "Guess which temperament was most commonly found among these successful people." After lively responses from the participants, he revealed that no one temperament stood out.

I found this tidbit of information interesting and even biblically consistent. First Corinthians 12 tells us the "body" is one member made of many parts. Not all can be an eye or an ear or a hand or a foot; instead, we are each to accept the function of each part.

Objective people realize that differentness among personalities is not only inevitable but desirable. They refuse to impose personal preferences upon others. While they may not have the same weaknesses as others, they have no reason to feel superior since they have other equally unique flaws.

Certainly Judy and I were different. Even I knew that.

Judy's upbringing was different, her values were different, and certainly her temperament was different.

Yet with all her differences and with all the problems they brought her, she had good things to offer too. She certainly was open to help, and she was willing to let others know her at a vulnerable level. She taught me that I could let my needs and feelings be known. She also showed that she could move forward even after experiencing difficulty.

When it was time for Judy to leave at the end of her second five-month stay, I rode in the car when Dad drove her to the bus station. I cried as I said good-bye and told her I hoped she got to come back again another time! To me, she was the greatest.

— 7 —

His Empathy:

The Story of Lazarus

John 11:1–36

WhenI was a boy in Sunday school, my teacher would occasionally ask individuals in the class to recite a favorite Bible verse. John 3:16 was the most popular, so someone (usually one of the girls) would raise a hand and recite it perfectly.

Me, I was into succinctness. I'd let someone else have the long verses and instead, I would quote John 11:35: "Jesus wept." The teacher could then move on to someone else, and I'd feel relieved that I would be asked no more questions.

Since then, I've learned to take the shortest verse in the Bible more seriously. In fact, it intrigues me. There in John's Gospel, those two words speak volumes to us! *Jesus wept.* Imagine that: Almighty God, reduced to tears. The Creator of everything, crying with His friend Mary. The One capable of unspeakable miracles, the One who commands the winds, standing in broad daylight, weeping. Why would this be?

In John 11 we read that Jesus was close friends with Lazarus, Mary, and Martha, residents of Bethany, just outside Jerusalem. Lazarus was a man of prominence, as evidenced by his formal burial place, and his two sisters were well liked and respected by many. It is easy to speculate that Jesus would stay in their home or enjoy a meal whenever He traveled to Jerusalem. Was Lazarus a family friend from childhood? Was he a financial supporter of Jesus' ministry? We don't know the answer to these questions, but we do know they had a special friendship.

So when Lazarus became very ill, near death, his sisters did the only thing they could do. They sent for Jesus. They had seen Him heal many times before. They certainly had faith in Him. Their only concern was in getting the word to Him quickly enough. Time was of the essence.

When the messenger brought word to Jesus, His disciples must have been startled by His response. Rather than saying, "Pick up your gear, fellows; we need to get to Lazarus quickly," He said the opposite: "Let's wait." Then He predicted that God's glory would be shown in this illness. Two days later, as they were preparing to leave,

Jesus informed the men that Lazarus was dead, but He would awaken him.

Put yourself in the disciples' shoes. They had been with Jesus for some time now, but they still hadn't figured Him out. Hadn't He seen the stress on the messenger's face? Why had He appeared so nonchalant about the whole thing?

By the time Jesus arrived on the outskirts of Bethany, Lazarus had been dead four days. The funeral was over. Many of the mourners had left. Mary and Martha had surely been disappointed that Jesus was not with them in their brother's final days. They had tried to console themselves by saying that He was a very busy man who could not just drop what He was doing to travel to their home. Nonetheless, they must have been hurt that He hadn't come in time to save their brother.

When the news came that Jesus was on the outskirts of town, Martha perked up. Setting aside her feelings of frustration, she hurried to Him and expressed belief. "Lord, if You had been here, my brother would not have died." Jesus then startled her by answering, "Your brother will rise again." Naturally Martha answered Him, "I know that he will rise again in the resurrection at the last day." She did not know that He meant immediately, and she did not wait for Him to tell her more. Instead, Martha went home to tell her sister, Mary, that Jesus had arrived. Martha was a woman of action.

Mary's personality was a stark contrast to her sister's. She was more contemplative. In another biblical scene we see her sitting at Jesus' feet, listening to His teachings, as

Martha prepares the food. Surely Mary had pondered His new ideas many times over in His absence. She was propelled by the craving to know Jesus intimately.

Imagine Mary's response to Lazarus's death. Family attachments were of utmost priority to her. She was a very loyal friend, and when she committed herself to a relationship, she was in it all the way. No doubt, she had enjoyed talking for hours with her brother about Jesus' mission and their belief in Him as Israel's Messiah.

Now Lazarus was gone. No more intimate conversations late at night. No more family gatherings built around lavish meals. No more laughter or hugs. It had all ended. Mary could hardly contain herself, and she was not shy in showing her hurt. She, too, had desperately hoped Jesus would appear for a last-minute healing. But regrettably He did not.

Then she heard the news: "Jesus is nearby and He wants to see you, Mary." It had been just a few days since the funeral, so her grief was fresh. A flood of thoughts must have spilled through her mind: *It will be so good to see Jesus. Lazarus talked about Him right up to the end. I just wish He could have been here a week ago. Where is He? I've got to see Him right away!*

Then the moment came when she saw her dear Friend in the distance, and she could hold in her emotions no more. She burst into tears when she recognized the compassion in Jesus' eyes. Her friends began crying as well. Though her vision was blurry now, she stepped up her pace so she could embrace Him.

Focus now on Jesus. He had come expectantly, knowing

how hearts would be softened when Lazarus would arise, prompting many to receive Him as their Messiah. But none of that was in His mind at this moment.

Only Mary. He knew how heartbroken she was at her brother's passing. He knew her well enough to know she had been confused by His absence. He had much to explain to her, and He knew how eagerly she would listen. But words would prove inadequate at this moment.

As John recorded this scene he explained that Jesus was deeply moved in spirit and was troubled. Then the two profound words: *Jesus wept.*

Why was He crying? The answer is clear. He had set aside His own mission for the moment and focused entirely on His friend's feelings. He felt her hurt and confusion as if it were His own. He had no need to speak to her; He only held her gently and let her cry as long as she needed. His tears communicated everything that needed to be said: *I'm with you, Mary. What you feel is what I feel. I want nothing more than for you to know that I'm by your side, sharing your emotions with you.*

I can imagine that several minutes passed before they finally spoke. He comforted her with understanding words, then told her as He had told Martha: He would still perform the miracle, even though it seemed too late.

Expressing Jesus' Empathy
to Others

Jesus responded to Mary with *empathy*, the capacity to experience another person's feelings and perceptions *from that person's point of view.* He was willing to suspend His own agenda so Mary could feel understood.

Can you relate to Mary's mood? Perhaps you've felt hurt or isolated. Maybe you've been angry, fearful, numb—all at the same instance. You've yearned for a best friend to turn to, and perhaps, like Mary, you've received some consolation, but not from that one person who could share everything with you. Then you see that special person, and words leave you. Instead, you respond with tears of enormous sorrow, of relief, of uncertainty. That's where Mary was.

And that's where Tammy was too. She's the woman I mentioned in Chapter 1 who was in church every time the doors opened and who had struggled for years with secret anger and insecurities. Yet she experienced the same stressors many other mothers face. Why was she feeling so blue? As I talked with this forty-year-old woman I realized she had become so caught up in her own feelings, she lost much of her ability to tune in to others. She and I had an interesting discussion about this.

"At first glance, you might say I am completely absorbed in my family's needs," Tammy commented. "Most of my day consists of doing things for someone else. Kids can be very demanding, and mine are no exception. But honesty requires me to admit that while I do all sorts of things for them, I don't necessarily think about their feelings.

"When my daughter or son becomes emotional, I just want to get them in line so they won't express themselves too disruptively."

Tammy told a story about correcting her ten-year-old daughter, Anna, who was fighting with a playmate. At that moment, all she could think of was: *Get Anna in line.* Her reaction turned into a disaster as her daughter accused her of not caring about her. In our time together, Tammy expressed a desire to know how to respond to others' emotions without making the immediate problem worse.

It was then that we examined several components that are necessary for us to be empathetic.

We Need to Let Emotions Run Their Course

Most people would admit they are ready solution-givers when others express their problems. That's what often happened as Tammy responded to her daughter.

Emotions need to be expressed freely so that efforts to resolve them can be pursued knowledgeably. If someone tells me he or she feels angry because of a friend's rejection, I need to take time to understand why this person feels so angry rather than immediately suggesting a solution. In doing so, I accomplish two things: My response will be better because I am more informed, and I show the person he or she has a privilege to feel this way.

Suppose your wife expresses regret that her friend had to cancel a luncheon engagement. You might reply, "Oh well, I guess you'll have to call her back and schedule another time." Or you could be empathetic. You could ask a delving question like, "I wonder why your friend keeps canceling luncheon engagements?"

Or when your son is dejected because of a poor grade,

you could reply, "Maybe next time you will be motivated to study hard like I've told you all along." Or you could be empathetic. You could note his genuine disappointment and say, "I can tell by the look on your face you weren't expecting that bad grade."

Our tendency to squash emotions even occurs when others try to share their positive feelings. If a friend enthusiastically tells us about getting a raise at work, we may respond with, "It's been a year since I got a raise," rather than celebrating the good news with the friend.

When empathy is our goal, we allow others to express their emotions. We can make reflective statements such as, "You've been waiting for that raise a long time! That's great!"

An empathetic person openly acknowledges that feelings are an integral part of who we are, and those feelings need to be fully explored.

Tammy admitted to me, "In seminars and instruction courses, I've heard many people talk about the difficulty men have in communicating on an emotional level. But I don't respond well to emotions myself. Sometimes emotions take longer to iron out than I want them to take. I want to move on to something more productive. I've decided that I am so focused on being productive, I sometimes lose sight of the relationships I want to develop."

Wanting her to capitalize on her insight, I asked, "What would be different if you became more tuned in to other people's emotions?"

"I'd communicate with more patience; that's for sure." Then she slowed her speech and remarked, "I wouldn't be in such a hurry to move the subject along." Another pause. "You know, my day is so driven by the next 'have-to' activity that my communication style has become driven as well. I need to let my family feel what they feel, and if it means we take a few moments longer in sifting out our circumstances, so be it."

Jesus was in no hurry to make Mary's grief go away. He powerfully illustrated how important she was to Him, and His willingness to let her emotions run their course made Him very influential in her life.

In order to be empathetic, we must let emotions run their course, and we must also set aside our own agendas, as Jesus did.

We Need to Set Aside Our Own Agendas

When Jesus returned to Bethany, He had a clear agenda to perform a resurrection miracle at the tomb of Lazarus. He could have seen His interactions with Martha and Mary as a distraction, but as Jesus demonstrated so many times, His agenda was never so important He could not slow down long enough to tune in to others.

Several years ago, an incident in my home illustrated how capable I was of shoving aside other people's feelings in order to maintain my self-important agenda. It was a typical evening in our house. I was in the den, preparing for a Bible class I would be teaching in a few days. My daughter, Cara, who was about six at the time, was in the kitchen, coloring an elaborate picture. As she finished she bounded into the den, held up the drawing, and shouted, "Daddy, look at my drawing!"

I peered at her over my reading glasses and replied, "Can't you see I'm reading something important? I'll be with you in a few minutes when I finish what I'm doing." Then I buried my head again in my book.

Out of the corner of my eye I watched Cara's smile disappear. Dejectedly she walked back to the kitchen, probably thinking either that her dad didn't care about her or that he was an insensitive jerk. That's when my guilt hit me. Here I was, reading this all-important literature about the Christian life, and I was so intent on getting my work done, I had become incapable of *living* the Christian life!

Immediately I called to Cara and asked, "What was it you wanted to show me?" She was back in the den in an instant, and her blue eyes lit up once more as she proudly displayed her masterpiece. We took four or five minutes to talk about this picture and the other drawings she had planned. I held her for a moment in my arms and told her how proud I was of her. Then she ran off, totally satisfied.

Was it hard for me to set aside my agenda for five minutes to tune in to my daughter's feelings? No. Was it natural for me to get away from my work to spend some time with her? Now that's a different story.

You will probably find it unnatural to be empathetic at times. As you think about your childhood you may remember your parents emphasizing work rather than relationships. More eleven-year-old children feel pressure from their parents to clean their rooms or to complete their homework assignments than to learn the ins and outs of their sibling's feelings.

As adults, then, we continue that trend. We learn what

the world of work requires of us, and we pursue it. We worry about the requirements of running the family schedule with some resemblance of order, and we give our attention to that.

But let's take a lesson from Jesus' style of interacting. Certainly He had many performance goals to accomplish. But above all, He wanted to communicate affirmation to people. By hearing individuals at their deepest level of feelings, He would establish this fact: *You are of utmost importance to Me.*

How about you? When are you most likely to ignore another person's emotional needs? What activities can so captivate your attention that you lose sight of the feelings of those near you? An honest evaluation will help you to be more empathetic.

Obviously, a willingness to be involved is also necessary before any of us can be truly empathetic.

We Need to Be Willing to Be Involved

Empathy is a step into another's personality, and therefore it implies a desire to be connected to that person. It means we will make an ongoing effort to know his or her preferences and quirks and reactions.

When I talk with busy people like Tammy, I often hear a common protest. She expressed it well: "You're saying I should be more involved? Dr. Carter, I've got so many involvements now, I don't know what to do with them. I don't think I could add any more."

Such a protest shows that this person has misinterpreted my meaning. I'm not talking about involvement in more activities; I'm referring to emotional involvement, which sometimes doesn't take a great deal of time.

Go back to that moment when I was giving the brush-off to my daughter, Cara. I became involved in her project, and it only cost me a few minutes. Yet it told her something enormously important: *You're important. What you feel matters. I'm interested in you.* After several more special moments like this, Cara knew her daddy cared about her in a very special way.

Emotional involvement doesn't mean you throw aside your own needs or you have to become an instant counselor. It simply shows that you see the inner issues behind the visible behaviors.

Emotional involvement requires creative communication because you will have to anticipate what must be going through the other person's mind. This will cause that person to feel as if your arm is around his or her shoulder while you are discussing the issue of the moment. Connectedness will occur.

I explained this to Tammy. Then I went on to add, "I find that when I am sharing an activity with someone, it is normal to swap stories about events. If someone talks about his or her child's preferences, I'll tell a similar story about Cara. Do you do that?"

"Constantly. Are you suggesting it's wrong to do that?"

"Not necessarily. But I *am* suggesting that before I switch subjects to talk about my issues, I need to stay with the other person a little longer. It would be a way of saying I care."

The incarnation of Christ is the supreme illustration of

personal involvement. Rather than remaining an abstract, unapproachable Being, Almighty God did the unthinkable. He stepped away from His throne room and took humanity in its fullness upon Himself. He experienced hunger pangs, He endured the common cold, He had to keep caught up on His sleep—just as we do. In doing so, He identified with us.

Finally, to show empathy, we need to openly display our understanding of another person's situation.

We Need to Openly Display Our Understanding

By now it should be apparent that empathy is more than simply saying, "I understand how you must feel." Empathy involves an open declaration of what you notice. For instance, to a dejected teenager who hangs up the phone after learning that social plans have been canceled, you might say, "I know how much you were looking forward to going out. This has to be a major disappointment."

A number of people ask, "But don't you think people just want to be left alone instead of having to talk about their feelings?"

To the contrary, I have found that the vast majority of people appreciate it when I make the effort to communicate *I see what is inside you.* I take the initiative with the assumption that a person will let me know if it is too uncomfortable for him or her. If that happens, I shift gears.

Several years ago a friend was hospitalized for viral encephalitis, an inflammation of the brain that can be very painful and potentially deadly. When I heard the news I immediately went to the hospital to see him and entered his room at the same time another friend arrived for a visit. Tom's room was dimly lit, and he was clearly in pain. Shortly into our conversation I remarked, "Tom, I'm certain this illness caught you off guard. How are you feeling about having to struggle with something so major?"

Before he could speak, the other friend interrupted, "You don't need to worry about those kinds of problems right now, Tom. . . . How's the food here in the hospital?" He carefully controlled the conversation in this way for several minutes; then he left. At that point, Tom turned to me and said, "Now, back to your question . . ." For several minutes we discussed his fears about the illness and his concern for his wife and children.

Tom needed to feel that he was not completely alone in his struggle to make sense of his predicament. He needed an empathetic listener. The other friend had assumed erroneously that it would be too stressful for Tom to discuss those feelings.

To prove that God does not want humans to function in machinelike precision, He gave us subjective reactions— emotions. We are living an empty life when we refuse to touch each other emotionally. Knowing this, Jesus freely spoke on the emotional level, especially in one-to-one situations.

As you contemplate the trait of empathy, think of the many ways you could improve your relationships by acknowledging others' feelings. And then watch how they respond to you.

THE RESPONSE TO EMPATHY

The apostle John does not leave any question about how Mary responded to Jesus. He records a time when Jesus was at the home of Lazarus several weeks later. Martha had prepared a meal for Him, and Jesus was enjoying conversation with Lazarus. Then Mary appeared with a vial of perfume that cost the equivalent of an average worker's yearly wage! Without a word, she opened it at Jesus' feet, lovingly washed them and caressed them with the oil, then dried His skin with her own hair. She knew she would raise questions in the minds of some, but she had thought and thought about how she could honor her Friend. This was the most unique way she knew to do it.

Just as you and I do, Mary had emotional ups and downs, and she had found Jesus receptive to her every expression. Her gift of perfume was her way of saying, *Thank You for touching my heart.*

That's what can happen when you incorporate empathy into your relationships. You draw others in with the message that says, *What you feel is what I sense. You make a difference to me.*

Let me conclude with another story about Cara. Five years after the incident I mentioned earlier, she and a friend bolted into the house, sweating profusely and breathing rapidly. As they stood in front of my chair, I widened my eyes and said, "What in the world is going on? You two look like you've seen a ghost!"

"It's worse than that, Dad! We've seen Ryan, and he won't leave us alone!"

Ryan was the neighbor who, like most twelve-year-old boys, displayed his affection by teasing the girls relentlessly. I suspect you have a Ryan in your neighborhood too.

Nodding slowly I replied, "Oh, so you've had a rough encounter with a boy, and it's got you feeling anxious. Sounds like we need to talk about this."

Hearing my response, Cara leaned over to her friend and said, "You've got to understand something about my dad. He likes to talk about my feelings, so we have these kinds of discussions when something goes wrong."

I just grinned at her explanation and thought to myself, *That's the nicest thing anyone has said about me all week!*

Be careful. If you offer empathy often enough, you'll get a reputation for it!

His Assertiveness:

Jesus and the Moneychangers

Mark 11:15–18; Luke 18:18–25; and Luke 19:45–48

W hen I was in graduate school a professor once asked me, "What makes you feel angry?"

I immediately thought, *I can't admit that I get angry. That wouldn't look good.* Back then it was very important for me to maintain an impeccable Christian reputation, so I was always reluctant to admit my humanness.

I smugly replied, "Well, I don't really feel angry much—maybe a little frustrated from time to time, but not angry." Surely, I thought, the professor would realize he was speaking to a cool, composed person who really had it together.

To my dismay, he persisted. "But Les, frustration *is* a form of anger, as is annoyance or irritability or impatience. Don't you feel those things?"

Uh-oh, I was caught now. Certainly I couldn't pretend to be that perfect. "Well, sometimes I suppose I do, but I try not to let it get out of hand." (It just about killed me to admit that I struggled with these emotions just like the rest of the human race.)

Twenty years later I've learned to drop the pretenses. I'll admit it. I can feel angry just as much as anyone else. I feel angry when the kids leave the back door open in midsummer. Or when the guy driving in front of me is a preoccupied slowpoke. Or when the dog uses our formal living room as her place of relief. Or when someone interrupts me when I'm speaking my opinions.

My *intention* is to eliminate my anger as much as possible, but I'm afraid I'm a long way from reaching that goal. I have the same human nature as anyone else, so I have moments when this emotion shows up whether or not I want it there. Our emotions are an inescapable part of our humanness. Only a robot (which is the way I once tried to live) can claim immunity from unpleasant feelings.

Do you know similar feelings of anger? It's okay. You can admit it, and I promise I won't throw stones at you. Maybe you are the kind of person who has episodes of anger that completely engulf you. Or you could be the type who struggles with smaller yet frequent episodes of irritability or impatience. Anger is shown in a wide array of behaviors. We can never completely avoid it, so it is best to acknowledge its presence by calling it what it is.

Did Jesus become angry? Absolutely. As you read Scripture you will recognize that He spoke words of rebuke when faced with self-centered or self-righteous people. He was not one to sit on His emotions when it was obvious that He needed to share His thoughts and feelings for someone else's benefit.

The most common example of Jesus' anger is His cleansing of the moneychangers from the temple. Because of the force of His expression, we often misunderstand His anger, so let's look carefully at this event.

The scene occurs during the Passover Week that culminated in Jesus' crucifixion and resurrection. Prior to entering the city, Jesus stood on top of a hill overlooking the enormous crowd that was pouring into Jerusalem for the holy festivities. A powerful surge of emotion overcame Jesus, and He wept with the agonizing cry of a person at a funeral. The sight of the people reminded Him of how oblivious most of them were to God's plan of redemption.

This feeling remained as Jesus made His way to the temple, the hub of activity where the true worship of God was supposed to occur. As He neared the temple grounds He was sickened by the sounds of the hucksters, who shouted like carnies at a modern-day fair. Merchants were selling animals for sacrifice—lambs for the wealthy visitors and doves for the common folk. Prices were ludicrously high, ensuring a tremendous profit for those on the take. But the merchants had rationalized their actions, saying, "Hey, we're doing these pilgrims a service, so what's the harm in making a few coins?" To add insult to injury, moneychangers were exchanging foreign currency into temple currency, and of course these folks were racking up a sizable profit too.

The noise level must have been tremendous. The smell of animals greeted Jesus as He stepped into the outer court, the court of the Gentiles. Then it happened. Jesus confronted a group of buyers and sellers, shouting, "It is written, 'My house is a house of prayer,' but you have made it a 'den of thieves'" (Luke 19:45).

Then He bolted over to the tables where the money-changers carefully guarded their piles of cash. Coins flew everywhere as He knocked over the tables. He did the same to the dove merchants. Some doves got loose and soared away quickly. The merchants scrambled to salvage what they could, and they probably had to compete with a few bystanders who were willing to pocket the loose money before the moneychangers could reclaim it.

When Jesus single-handedly shut down business in the courtyard, an eerie silence must have ensued. The people knew they were in the presence of an influential person. Many of them surely applauded inwardly, thinking, *Finally, someone has had the nerve to express what I've felt for years.* It must have been quite a day!

What was Jesus trying to accomplish with His anger? Remember it flowed from the agonizing grief He had felt as He looked down on the people coming into Jerusalem who were missing the message of God's love. His anger was not meant to be a macho display of force. Rather, His intent was to clearly communicate His convictions about what displeased the Father. A mild statement of His beliefs would have been ignored amidst the noise and distractions of the temple courtyard.

Not all of Jesus' moments of assertiveness were accompanied by a use of force. Earlier in their ministry, the disciples had been turned away by a village of Samaritans who did not want to give them travel provisions. Angered, James and John suggested that Jesus command fire to drop from heaven to consume these people. Jesus must have felt disgusted by the Samaritans' rejection, but He was also annoyed by the disciples' malicious request. He chided them for their spitefulness and encouraged them to move on to a friendlier town. This time He handled His frustration by teaching His followers a higher principle and then moving on to a more palatable environment.

When most of us feel angry, we are uncertain about the best path to take. Should we just accept the circumstances? Should we directly confront the person?

Jesus knew there were times when it was necessary to assert His views, yet He knew when to state His boundaries more gently—and when to leave well enough alone.

To determine whether anger can get the best of you, think about how many of these situations pertain to you:

- When reprimanding another person, I have been known to speak with irritability or criticism.

- I can become moody when things are not going well;
  it is best to stay out of my way at that point.
- When someone does not react well to my expression
  of frustration, my annoyance can get out of control.

If you responded to any of these statements, don't be alarmed. We all have moments when our anger is funneled in the wrong direction. To formulate a plan to manage our anger, we must first understand what it is.

WHAT IS ANGER?

Anger is our emotion of self-preservation, which propels us to stand up for our self-respect, our heartfelt needs, our rock-solid convictions. Many of us have seen the ill effects of poorly managed anger, so we readily conclude that anger is to be avoided at all cost. Others proclaim that anger is good, a necessary reaction to ward off unpleasant intrusions.

Let's stay away from either extreme. Though anger can indeed have devastating repercussions, it is not always bad. And though it may address our violated rights, we can use it to manipulate others. A balanced perspective reminds us that anger should only be used for constructive purposes. When that happens, it is called *assertiveness*.

ASSERTIVENESS: CONSTRUCTIVE ANGER

I have been asked, "Do I have a right to be assertive with

my anger?" My response is to throw out the word *right,* which can involve selfish desires, and replace it with the word *responsibility.* Now ask the question again: "Do I have a responsibility to be angry?" Sounds different, doesn't it?

Sometimes it would be irresponsible to assert your feelings or beliefs. Perhaps the subject is too minor, or maybe the timing is wrong. You might be seen as bossy or critical if you are assertive too often. Yet there are times when assertiveness can prompt a person to be more considerate. It can help clear the air of potential grudges. It can promote teamwork.

One of the things I like most about my counseling practice is that I can share with others the insights I receive. I worked with one woman, Emily, who was struggling to figure out this balance.

Emily, a forty-four-year-old mother of nine- and fifteen-year-old girls, often felt pushed to the limits by their demands. Her husband, Gary, was fairly active as a dad, but not very aware of his wife's needs, so he and Emily bickered frequently.

"My problem," Emily told me, "is that I go from one extreme to the other. Sometimes I just hold things inside and fume because my family doesn't understand how to meet my needs. Other times I snap and growl, and when I do, it sets off easy arguments that ruin an entire evening. I'm at a loss to know what to do."

She told me her father would rage at the drop of a hat. She feared him and determined never to do anything that might set him off. Her mother was quite the opposite. She catered to her dad and was very quiet. The mother rarely spoke out about her needs and instructed Emily to do whatever was necessary to keep the peace. The mother was susceptible to some mild episodes of depression, but at least she never exploded. "She was the most mild-mannered woman you'd ever meet," Emily said.

In our first session, Emily was caught off guard when I asked her to tell me her philosophy for handling her anger. A stunned look crossed her face as she replied, "It's never occurred to me that anyone could have a philosophy of handling emotions. I just let them run their course."

Emily gave me some examples of how she handled irritations. "When my fifteen-year-old gets on the phone she can talk forever, and she has friends galore. We even got a second phone line, but it still bothers me when she stays on the phone too long. When I talk with her about it, she doesn't like what I have to say, so our conversations quickly deteriorate into an argument."

"What is another example of anger that goes sour?"

"Well, my husband is more perfectionistic than I am. To some extent that's fine because he helps keep me organized. But when he criticizes me about things like my housecleaning or my scheduling of activities, it really bugs me. I've learned I can't out-debate him, so I often hold in my anger. I know it makes me appear moody, but I don't know what else to do."

Jesus never responded to people's needs in exactly the same way. While He knew that strong words were necessary for the temple merchants, He only chided His disciples for their anger at the Samaritans. We can learn to be assertive rather than angry by using several general guidelines. First, consider your reputation.

Consider Your Reputation

One reason Jesus could afford to speak so powerfully to the temple merchants was His reputation as a peacemaker, a healer, a teacher, and a servant. This episode was not part of an ongoing habit of creating a major ruckus. People who witnessed the temple cleansing had already seen or heard of His unusual godliness.

What is your reputation? Are you known for excessive criticism or a tendency to rage or to lecture? Or are you known as being insensitive or aloof?

If so, you will need to establish a reputation for fairness, kindness, and consideration. It would help to be known as a good listener and as one who is not judgmental or rude. Only then can you expect to be taken seriously.

When I talked with Emily about this matter, it struck a raw nerve. "Oh, Dr. Carter, I'm afraid my girls see me more as a drill sergeant than as an approachable mom," she admitted. "I care about them deeply, but I spend so much time nagging and correcting them, I'm afraid they don't see that side of me."

"Why do you suppose that happens?"

"It all seems to boil down to time. We are so rushed at our house that we seem to be constantly running from one event to the next. Stacie, my oldest, was elected cheerleader earlier this year, so she is always on the go with school-related activities. Missy is very popular with her friends, and she likes having them over a lot."

I nodded as I listened. "So you work yourself into easy agitation as you prod them to move from here to there, and before you know it, annoyances pop up left and right."

"That's the picture! My girls are sweet, but they're also very disorganized. I'm constantly picking up after them or urging them to clean things up before they move on to the next activity. The result is chronic bickering."

Emily and I decided that she and her girls needed to set aside time three or four days a week just to talk—on Saturday mornings or before bedtime on weeknights. She needed to show them she could actually be easygoing. They needed to laugh together, to share feelings, to discuss problems.

What could you do to bond with those you speak assertively to? Could you develop a greater willingness to pass out compliments? Could you take time pressures less seriously? Could you listen more actively?

Once you establish a caring reputation, you need to be careful to speak without pleading and coaxing.

No Pleading or Coaxing

In studying Jesus' interactive style, I have noticed a lack of one trait. He was not coercive. When He had something important to say, He never used a pleading tone of voice. He would clearly state His boundaries, then let people make their own choices. When He responded to the rich young ruler's question about entering His kingdom, the young man walked away (see Matt. 19:16–30). But Jesus did not chase after him. He allowed the young man to make his own decisions.

Too often we can step across the boundaries of healthy assertiveness by pushing good ideas too strongly. We not only present our feelings or facts or preferences, we do so with a loud or coercive voice. When we communicate this way, we invite a power play that will invariably turn sour.

Emily told me about an argument she had with her husband, Gary. "There are times when Gary tunes me out to the extent that I feel very isolated. He just doesn't respond when I ask him for help around the house or if I express a concern. He gives me excuses and entirely misses what I'm asking."

"So that's when the arguing occurs?"

"Yes. Last night I started crying and raising my voice. I wanted him to know how much I need him to support me. 'We only have a limited time with our children,' I told him, 'and I need you to be more of a team player.' But I'm afraid I spoke so strongly he couldn't hear my words."

Nodding slowly I replied, "Boy, it's sure easy for our anger to quickly carry us away before we even realize what's happening." Then, pointing to my throat, I said, "Our most important tool of communication is right here. Our tone of voice sets the stage for others' ability to hear us. If we are too overbearing too often, we lose influence. It's important to keep our tone of voice at a pitch where it implies firmness *and* respect."

When we speak assertively, we still need to be mindful that others are not obliged to agree with us or to change just because we want them to. People differ widely in the way they view the world, and what seems perfectly logical to one person may be ludicrous to another.

Assertiveness can be guided by what I call "no-hooks communication." This means that the words spoken will be clearly stated but without excessive efforts to force others to agree. When I suggested this concept to Emily, she protested, "But that might backfire. If I speak less persuasively to Gary he might ignore me altogether. *Then* where would we be?"

"I suppose you'd be no worse off than you are now," I replied.

Can you think of some common instances when you could exchange assertive speech for angry communication? Consider the following examples:

- Your spouse has forgotten (again) to follow through on the favor you asked. You can choose to give an accusing speech about the necessity of cooperation in a family, or you can choose to quietly, but firmly, state how important that favor was to you. What would you do?

- Your child does not see the merit in keeping his or her room clean, no matter how many times you try to elicit the child's cooperation. You can gripe about your being the child's indentured servant, or you can calmly and succinctly explain the consequences of keeping a messy room.

- Your employer expects more from you than you are reasonably able to deliver. You can plead your case

to him or her, or you can let your boss know that you
will finish all that can be done in a day's work, then
let him or her decide what to do about the rest. Would
you be so bold?

Your job is to speak the truth as fairly as possible, then
let go of any coercion.

It's often easier to avoid pleading or coaxing if we
recognize our limits.

Recognize Your Limits

Most people have no problem admitting their obvious
limits. I don't mind admitting that my athletic talents are
limited; I will never be a Roger Staubach. Likewise, my
musical skills are limited; I'll never be a Pavarotti.

Yet I hate to admit some other limits. I'm limited in my
capacity to maintain perfect composure. I'm limited in my
ability to change my wife's mind or to make the kids
understand my reasons for setting boundaries. I know
these things to be true, but honestly accepting them means
I'll have to admit my lack of control.

If I cannot force someone to think just like I think, I will
have to accept that he or she might think illogically at times
(according to my version of logic, that is). I don't like that.
My distaste for this conclusion causes me to ignore my
limits.

This concept was difficult for Emily to accept. In her
eagerness to encourage Gary to help her, she was denying
her limits. "Emily, you're wanting to believe that all you
have to do is say the right words and you can make Gary
adjust. That's a denial of reality.

"I can understand that it won't be easy to admit that you genuinely cannot make things right," I reflected. "But let's look positively at something. Once you admit your limits, it frees you from much of your resentment and inner tension. You can choose to get out of the way and let the Holy Spirit take His rightful place rather than trying to play that role yourself. Recognizing your limits can result in a deeper resolve to rely more fully on God."

"I suppose it boils down to the question of whether I can trust God to be wholly God," she said. "It's embarrassing to admit, but I guess my anger implies that I've wanted to be God."

"You're not alone," I reassured her. "Every person struggles with the same desire. Our sinful nature is such that we each have unwarranted aspirations to be in control, and even though we can eventually admit that that control is an illusion, we struggle against ourselves. It will always be that way as long as we are on this side of heaven."

In addition to recognizing our limits, another way to be assertive rather than coercive is to avoid dumb questions.

Avoid Dumb Questions

When we become angry, a sense of desperation can push us to ignore rules of fair play and search for an angle that will help us gain the upper hand. A common pitfall is asking questions that are meant for anything *other* than gaining information.

Suppose you say to your daughter, "You need to clean up the mess in your bedroom." That's a fair request, one she should readily follow, right? But suppose she decides to piddle and stall. Here it comes, a dumb question: "What did I tell you to do just fifteen minutes ago?"

Or suppose you've talked to your wife about coordinating your schedules for the weekend, but later that day you realize she has been preoccupied with other issues. Here it comes, another dumb question: "Why can't I count on you to make a couple of simple phone calls? What's so hard about being organized?"

These questions have nothing to do with understanding the other person better or with gaining insights. They are purely guilt-inducing . . . and they are an invitation to argue. The unspoken, covert message is, *You're clearly not on the same level of intelligence as I am, you oaf.* Nonproductive questions undermine a person's self-respect.

As Emily reflected on her own tendency to ask such questions, she remarked, "But how else can I say it? If my girls won't clean up their rooms, I've somehow got to get them to obey."

"Drop the questions and make a statement that clearly reflects your desire. For instance, you could say 'Fifteen minutes ago I asked you to clean your room and the request still stands.' If that doesn't work, you can explain the consequences (noncoercively); then let the consequences communicate for you.

"Be succinct, then move on," I suggested. "In most cases the more you talk, the less the person listens to you."

I am not saying you should never ask questions, however. Good questions help us to:

- become more understanding ("Can you tell me why science is so boring for you?"), and
- become more insightful or introspective ("Why do you seem irritable when I bring up the subject of my brother?").

Good communication stimulates an open sharing of what we believe and feel.

Finally, we will be assertive rather than coercive if we determine the message's importance.

Determine the Message's Importance

Have you ever made a big deal over trivia? I know I have . . . too many times. It's an easy trap to fall in. I call this the "nearsighted syndrome." We can focus so intently on minor matters, we fail to put them in the perspective of the larger picture.

Emily admitted this error. "There are too many instances when I let minor matters get under my skin. When my kids leave their clothes on the floor or if my husband is a few minutes late, it can eat away at me. I know these things are unimportant in the long run, but I don't know how to keep them from becoming major nuisances to me. So how do I get to a point of balance?"

"On minor matters, the general rule of thumb is to state your preferences once, without coercion, then be willing to drop it. Only if a moral or ethical issue emerges should you really get firm. For instance, teaching your children to have a clean room is good, so be willing to speak openly on that issue. But also be aware that most kids are not meticulous, so you will have to accept that. If your children defy your preferences in a way that challenges your authority as a parent, it becomes a moral issue. At that point you may need to press your point more strongly by putting consequences on them if they do not obey."

There are times when you may feel you have been assertive, yet you *still* do not get any results. Others may simply have different priorities, or worse, they may not care about your needs or feelings. At this point, what do you do?

Some refuse to let up. They think, *I'm not getting anywhere now, but if I keep up the pressure I might make the breakthrough I want.* They proceed to push and push and push their point of view. Others may not be as openly persistent, but they drop into a wishful-thinking mode. *Why can't he understand what I'm saying?* they might wonder. *I just wish he would come to his senses and make the right adjustments.* These people set themselves up for bouts with depression and bitterness as they concoct dreams about utopian conditions that will never occur.

Let's face it. Some people simply will not make desirable changes, or they may not comprehend why we think as we do. As a result, they may be a permanent burr under the saddle.

Handling anger is not a black or white matter. Sometimes we need to know when and how to speak out for the good of a relationship; other times we need to know when to accept and leave it in God's hands. All of us will spend a lifetime trying to find and keep that balance.

His Respect:

The Story of Zacchaeus, the Tax Collector

Luke 19:1–10

A s I stepped into the waiting room to meet Joe for the first time, it was clear he did not want to be there. He made no eye contact with me, he responded to my handshake with a limp grip, and he walked sluggishly to my office. Then he plopped down in the nearest chair and slouched forward with his chin propped in one hand. Slender, in his late thirties, he was dressed nicely enough in a blue shirt with a loosened pinstriped tie. But his demeanor said loudly, *I sure wish you'd leave me alone, you clown.*

Joe had been sent to me by the family court system because he had been caught sexually molesting his thirteen-year-old stepdaughter and was known to have done the same to another girl. Like it or not, he had to see me for six months of weekly therapy.

So there we sat.

I asked him to give me the details of his misdeeds, and he told me how he had preyed upon the girl several times and how he wished her mother hadn't walked in when she did—all in very bland tones as if he were talking about the weather. I was struck by his complete lack of emotion or remorse. He seemed to be sorrier that he had been caught than repentant for what he had done.

Inside, my anger was building. I thought of how his actions could affect someone like my own daughter, Cara. I thought of the many grown women who had told me about past sexual abuse that had thrown them into tremendous confusion for many years and had finally led to extensive counseling. Now a man who had caused all that pain was sitting here with me, acting casual about something profoundly destructive.

It seemed impossible to relate to him or give him the respect necessary to help him. I'm sure Jesus must have felt the same way about Zacchaeus, a tax collector in the city of Jericho.

THE LITTLE TAX MAN IN JERICHO

In Jesus' day, tax collectors were not regulated by the same codes and laws that apply today. Taxation was wide open to fraud and abuse, and the Jews had to pay several taxes. Roman officials, who were disliked by the fiercely independent Jews because they considered them to be bullying intruders, systematically collected the first kind of tax—personal and property taxes. Through the years the Jews learned to tolerate them if for no other reason than the improved roads and waterways.

The Jews also had to pay another kind of tax, which brought even more openly contemptuous feelings: the commerce tax. A person buying or selling goods would be stopped at various intervals while traveling in and out of town to pay a customs tax on his or her goods. At a place as far off from Rome as Palestine was, this task was delegated to locals who were expected to collect an acceptable amount; they were allowed to keep anything they might collect beyond that reasonable fee. This led to almost unlimited opportunities for a money-hungry collector to exploit a powerless commoner.

As you would imagine, a Jew who accepted a job as a tax collector had to be motivated by sheer greed to make large sums of money and calloused to the point of complete disdain for his fellow countrymen's financial plight. Predictably, the Jews scorned these tax collectors as traitors and ostracized them from many of the activities in the community. Yet their craving for money and power was so great, they thrived on the notoriety that came with the job. Often they responded to public scorn with an equal hatred.

Zacchaeus was not only a tax gatherer, he was the chief tax man in Jericho. And if you had to be a tax gatherer, Jericho, just a dozen or so miles east of Jerusalem, was certainly the place to be. Near fertile, tree-lined fields, it was a crossroads for commerce going to and from Jerusalem; there was a steady flow of business, guaranteeing good profits for the tax trade. Also, many of the faithful made regular treks to the Holy City, and they had to pass through Jericho.

To have made it to the top in such a ruthless profession, Zacchaeus had to have been the kind of man who would shove his own mother aside if it might get him an advancement or two. He had amassed an incredible personal fortune, although it had probably meant excommunication from the church and being disowned by his own family.

On Jesus' final journey into Jerusalem He passed through Zacchaeus's hometown. Luke 19 tells us that the crowd there was enormous, partly because other travelers were also en route to Jerusalem and partly because they had heard that the Miracle Worker was nearby. People stopped their routine for a chance to see the celebrity from Nazareth.

Zacchaeus had heard the stories about the unbelievable healings, so he was just as eager to see Jesus as the next guy. But since Jesus' passing through Jericho was spontaneous, Zacchaeus's money could not buy him a favorable viewing spot. He had to scramble like the rest of the crowd, and because of his short stature he had to climb a tree like a kid and perch on one of its branches.

Why Jesus picked this man to converse with, no one knows for sure. He may have already known of Zacchaeus by reputation, or He may have met him previously through His disciple, Matthew. Or it may have been a chance encounter. The one thing we know for sure is that Jesus saw through Zacchaeus's phony pride and showed him something Zacchaeus had seen little of: respect.

As usual, the crowd was pressing against Jesus when He stopped beneath the tree holding the diminutive man. Surely the tax gatherer felt embarrassed as his anonymity within the crowd was immediately stripped away. He had never shown himself to be vulnerable, but there he was, sitting high up in that tree like a schoolboy waiting for a parade. Nonetheless, he was intrigued by this Prophet and curious to know why He would stop to speak to him.

Jesus' call to Zacchaeus was simple. He said, in effect, "Zacchaeus, why don't you get out of the tree and show Me where you live? I'd like to eat lunch with you."

Can't you hear the moan that went up from the crowd? "Oh, Jesus. Don't do that! That guy's a jerk!"

Yet Jesus ignored the crowd's and His disciples' sentiments and followed an eager Zacchaeus to his home. I'd be fascinated to know what they talked about. Zacchaeus probably did what most of us do when we entertain a first-time guest. He showed Jesus items of interest in his house, perhaps some carvings from Egypt or paintings from Persia he had picked up in his business. They may have talked about the economy or the burden of living under Roman rule. Perhaps he told Jesus of his history: where he grew up and how he had become employed as a government worker.

But at some point, Jesus took over the conversation. He sensed that this man hungered for something more substantial than money, so He talked about Zacchaeus's need for God's presence. "Zacchaeus, I care about you and your well-being. Let Me share with you how you can have true joy." The visit probably lasted several hours. Surely Zacchaeus made provisions for the disciples to be fed, so they were probably in no great hurry to leave.

This man really does care about me, Zacchaeus must have thought. *He's not impressed by my possessions yet I think He actually likes me!*

Jesus knew the craving for respect that had driven Zacchaeus into this lifestyle, yet respect, the acknowledgment of his worth, was the one thing Zacchaeus had never received.

How capable are you of giving the gift of respect? If you are like me, you find it easy to respect people when they deserve it. But what about the moments when those others are less than wonderful? Can you still muster respect for them?

I certainly had difficulty doing so as I listened to Joe speak so complacently about his abuse of his stepdaughter and another young girl. Instead of being respectful, I wanted to reach across the room, grab the guy by his shirt, and shout, "Wake up, fellow! Can't you grasp for just one moment how you have hurt those girls?"

Then the thought occurred to me, *I'm the end of the road for this man. If I don't reach him, it's likely no one else will.* So at that moment I breathed a prayer: *Lord, I commit myself to giving this man respect, which is totally unnatural to me. Let Your grace be shown in his life.*

At the end of our first visit, I said, "Joe, since we have six months together, we might as well make the most of it." I asked him to make an inventory of the things in himself that he would like to change. "I'll help you sort them out, but you will have to take responsibility for our time together."

As the weeks passed, I was pleasantly surprised at Joe's response to my challenge. He began sharing his insecurities, his incredible feelings of loneliness and neediness, his anger. It was no shock to learn that he had had a very difficult childhood. Neglected for long stretches of time by his parents, he had dreamed about love yet felt inadequate to experience it. His peers had ostracized him in his youth, he had suffered a disastrous marriage and divorce, and now he was very unhappy in his current marriage.

One of the most common problems I see in counseling is the struggle with anger, especially anger that appears when others are showing a lack of respect. Most people are inclined to respond with a similar show of disrespect. At that point, relationships go downhill, with no one taking the necessary initiative to put respect at the center of the relationship.

How can we learn to incorporate into ourselves the ability to show respect to others, even when it's not easy?

SHOWING JESUS' RESPECT TO OTHERS

Jesus was certainly angered or frustrated when people derided Him or displayed ignorance or argued about petty matters. In spite of such improprieties, He understood that we all possess value. His task was to draw out that worth and show it to individuals so they could see themselves that way.

Who in your life needs to be respected? If you are married, your mate needs to sense your appreciation for his or her dignity. Your children also need to hear in your voice that you care about their perceptions, feelings, and activities. This is especially true when you are the disciplinarian.

If you are a single adult, you can have a powerful impact on other singles as you choose to uphold another person's dignity, never stooping to the tendency to exploit him or her sexually for your own gain. At your place of business, you can develop a reputation for being fair-minded and willing to speak kindly to co-workers, no matter how high or low they are on the ladder.

Contrary to popular opinion, respect does not have to be earned first. You can choose to give respect. It represents a commitment to recognize the sacredness of another person's God-decreed value.

Let's look at some key ingredients of respect.

Firmness without Condescension

It can be healthy and responsible to speak about our needs *as long as* we do so in a manner that upholds the dignity of the other person. For instance, it would be safe to say that Jesus was offended by the tax collector's willingness to exploit commoners. Yet, when He was inside Zacchaeus's home, I doubt that Jesus chewed him out royally. Did He address the issue of fairness? Of course.

During the visit, Zacchaeus made an important decision. He decided to do the fair thing and make restitution to the people he had cheated. With no pressure from the Master, he determined to return fourfold any money he had improperly taken from his fellow townspeople; furthermore, he offered to disperse 50 percent of his possessions to people in need. He would never be the same.

In His dealings with Zacchaeus, Jesus showed that strong convictions can be addressed while also maintaining respect. We could cite many examples of how this works:

- When a husband speaks to his wife about financial concerns, he chooses not to resort to a preaching tone of voice. Instead, he is steady in his words and knows when to stop his argument.

- When a mother corrects her daughter about her back-talking ways, she does so without fire in her eyes. She reminds her of the consequences of her behavior and gives the idea time to settle into the girl's mind.

- As a single man speaks to his friends about his breakup with a long-time girlfriend, he realizes it would be counterproductive to speak critically about her. He doesn't let his feelings justify rudeness.

Though we may genuinely believe our perceptions or beliefs are indeed better than the other person's, we can still operate on the conviction that we have no more or no less value as a person than anyone else.

In one of my discussions with Joe, he revealed a struggle common to many. "Sometimes I feel like I ought to stand up for myself when others are ignoring or belittling me, but I just hold my emotions inside. Then, after putting up with foul treatment for a while, I explode. I'm asking for respect, but the way I communicate that need is so foul, I don't get what I want."

"Joe, I wonder if you could learn to speak what is on your mind right away. Then you won't have a long emotional buildup, and you can talk in a more even tone of voice."

"That would be nice if I could just train myself to do it." A look of relief crossed his face.

"The key is to remember that you are a person of God-given value speaking to another person of God-given value." I knew this concept was very foreign to him, but I also knew he could change.

Analyze your own communication patterns. Do you also resort to the power tactics of a harsh voice or the silent treatment? Do you really *have* to get in the last word? Remember, people will respond less to your words than to your manner.

Practice Delicate Detachment

It is difficult to genuinely acknowledge another's worth and still remain emotionally aloof. Yet respect requires a certain amount of detachment. If that seems contradictory, think it through carefully. A man may realize that his brother-in-law does not think he is fit to be in their family. The brother-in-law criticizes him behind his back and treats him with indifference. Though this is a very undesirable situation, this man can remain detached from the brother-in-law by choosing not to respond in kind. He can speak civilly to the brother-in-law. This does not mean he denies his feelings, but he practices a delicate detachment.

When people have experienced major rejection (divorce, past abuse, unfair business dealings) it is very unnatural to let go. We tend to stay tied to other people through our resentments of those who have mistreated us.

It is false to say, "I can never respect a person who treats me with scorn." You may be inhibited from having any feeling of closeness, but you can choose not to succumb to bitterness or unnecessary competitiveness.

It did not take long for Joe's initial veneer of apathy to crack. As he talked more freely about his past, he cried readily. He expressed the guilt and remorse I did not see during his first visit; I realized his initial casualness had been a poor cover for his fears and shame. Joe told me he wanted to be different, but he was not sure he had the strength to change.

After several months, Joe said something to me that made me realize that all my efforts to expound upon insights and concepts were of secondary importance. He told me, "Les, I have to confess that I have a hard time understanding you. I've told you more about myself than I've ever told anyone, and most of it has been ugly. Yet, each time I come here you're kind to me. You've never scorned me or put me down. I've been waiting for that to happen, and I wouldn't blame you if you hated me. But it hasn't come. I find that to be totally amazing, and I appreciate it greatly."

Tears came to my eyes. I thought about that first visit and my reaction to him. I remembered my prayer and how I had to struggle to give him respect. I told Joe about this, and I reminded him he needed to accept that his value before God was real, no matter what sins he had committed. We discussed his need for the Savior and his need to be daily yielded to the Holy Spirit's direction. As I spoke, Joe cried like a child.

I learned something about myself through my interactions with Joe. I am not the most effective when I wax eloquently about brilliant theories but when I show respect to someone who needs it desperately.

His Reflective Thinking:

Jesus and the Elders in the Temple

Luke 2:40–52

Like every Jewish boy, Jesus had looked forward to His twelfth birthday and the Passover Feast after that because He would finally get to accompany His parents on their annual visit to the Holy City.

This was no ordinary trip. It was truly an event, a rite of passage into manhood. And now that day was here.

There was much noise and excitement on the morning Jesus and His parents left home. Most of the townspeople were going to Jerusalem for the festivities, so you can imagine the crowd congregating in the center of town, their bags packed with the necessary food and clothes for a two- or three-week trip. The donkeys carried much of this burden, but the men also wore backpacks. Those staying behind gave hugs and well wishes to the faithful who, like Joseph and Mary, made the familiar southbound journey year after year.

Young Jesus was not immune to the excitement that gripped the contingent of Nazarenes on their way to the big city. Yet He had never been to Jerusalem, at least not in His memory. He had heard all the stories of how big the buildings were, of food markets that stretched on and on, of the people from foreign countries speaking so many different languages, of the temple priests and their special clothing. He had heard some details of the animal sacrifices and had been warned that He should not have a weak stomach as He witnessed His first. He was told there were many itinerant teachers who, along with the Jerusalem scholars, had interesting, if not always credible, things to say about God and the law. He knew there was much to observe and absorb, and He was ready to stay as close to the action as He could be.

When scores, perhaps hundreds, of people travel in one group, you just cannot make good time. The organizers knew this, so they planned to pace themselves and allow several days each way. No one minded the time it took because it gave them a chance to visit with each other, some for the first time since the prior year's journey. Besides, all roads heading into Jerusalem were crowded with pilgrims who were also leaving their businesses behind for the annual festivities. The Nazarenes would stay together as best as they could, but they would also be rubbing shoulders with folks from Cana, Madon, Nain, and many other towns in their region.

Jesus probably began the journey walking beside Joseph and Mary, but after a while He likely wandered away to be with other boys from the synagogue school. He probably also talked to His friends' parents, asking about their past travels to Jerusalem, probing their understanding of the significance of the festivals as well as facts about the specific activities. Certainly He was admired by the entire Nazareth group as He had developed a reputation as a responsible, well-mannered young man. So when He talked with any one of them, they did not mind His curiosity; in fact they were stimulated by it. People rightly pegged Him as one who would go far, perhaps as a teacher or a town leader.

Once the Nazarene contingent arrived at Jerusalem, they spread out in temporary living places. Most stayed in small, inexpensive inns; others moved in with friends and relatives, and still others camped out. Joseph and Mary would be there a solid week, and they knew they could not possibly keep up with the eager adolescent. So they said, "We know You want to go to the temple to see what's happening there, and that will be fine. We'll be here each evening if You need us. Just take care of Yourself."

Surely Jesus walked admiringly through some of the

beautiful gardens of the city. He sought out and found Herod's palace and gawked at its splendor. He stopped to eat the food sold in street-side vendors' booths. And He was probably taken aback by the number of beggars who dramatically cried to Him, hoping for some pity from the naive newcomer in town.

But the place Jesus wanted to see most was the temple, His Father's house. When He first came upon it He probably gazed in amazement, awed by its palatial beauty as it sat majestically above the grand city. He walked almost reverently as He made His way up the steps and through the various courts: the court of the Gentiles, the court of women, the court of men of Israel and the priests, and then the actual temple itself. All the way, He recalled many of His synagogue-school lessons, which had explained the purpose and function of each section. He probably wondered to Himself how many of His fellow Jews knew or cared about the significance of this great structure.

Occasionally He stopped and listened to a teacher who felt called to expound upon some truth related to God's law. Jesus learned quickly that some of these men were looked upon skeptically, even with derision, while others were held in high esteem. He wanted to hear and absorb what each one believed, whether or not He could agree with what He heard.

Soon He found His way into the teaching circles of the academic celebrities, the scholars who looked forward to Passover Week because it gave them the opportunity to communicate their wisdom to large audiences. Some were pompous publicity seekers; others genuinely wanted to be enlightening. In spite of the large crowds they would attract each day, Jesus was small enough to work His way to the center of the circle of listeners so He could see and hear everything. He had many questions, but the enormity of the crowds prohibited Him from freely talking with the instructors. He would return each evening to Joseph and Mary, speaking excitedly about what He had heard. Then, first thing the next morning, He would be off again to hear the teachers lecture on subjects about God and His dealings with the Jewish nation through the centuries.

The quality that propelled Jesus' curiosity was His reflective thinking. The young Jesus wanted to get into the trenches and go through the exercise of discovering truth, rather than merely being told what He should believe.

Becoming a Reflective Thinker

Are you a reflective thinker? Have you formulated a cohesive philosophy of life? Can you withstand moments of doubt?

Many people make their way to my counseling office because they have hardly ever reflected upon their philosophy of life. As a result, they collapse when difficulties come because they have few inner resources to draw upon. One such person was Philip.

In his mid-thirties, Philip was a college-educated professional who worked at a good job that allowed him to live a suburban, middle-class lifestyle. Philip had many outer trappings of happiness, but inwardly he was not satisfied.

"I've had one problem after another throughout my entire life," he told me. "My mother was impossible to live with. She drove my dad away when I was ten, and my younger brother and I had to live with her ranting and raving day after day. No one will confirm it but I think she had an affair that led to the end of her marriage. Anyway, Dad wanted nothing to do with her, and my brother and I had little contact with him for the rest of our childhood."

Philip explained further that he had struggled to keep friends, both as a kid and as an adult. Like his father, he had been divorced and remarried. "Living with women is a chore," he told me. He said he and his current wife, Joanie, had argued frequently in their first two years of marriage, but this eventually subsided when Philip decided it was useless to discuss matters with her.

One day Philip expressed a frustration that gave me a clear understanding of his ongoing distress. He complained, "Every time I come in here I feel like you want me to look at my inner motivation for being the way I am. When are we going to talk about what my family ought to be doing to make my life easier?"

"As soon as they come in here to discuss their problems," I replied. I was not being flippant in my response. I had told Philip in the first session that if his wife were willing to come to counseling I would welcome her, and I had also said we would look at ways to alter his communication with his parents. They, too, were welcome in my office.

"You know that's not going to happen," Philip replied. "Joanie says I'm the one with the problem. She doesn't feel the need to expose her feelings to a stranger. And my parents wouldn't set foot in here if you paid them. It's very unfair that they point the finger at me and tell me I've got to be the one who restructures my personality."

I nodded in agreement. "Anytime one person is hurting, other people in the family also have problems. So I agree; it would be good if they delved into the same soul-searching you're doing. But apparently that's only wishful thinking at this point. Right or wrong, the burden is on your shoulders."

Was I being insensitive to suggest that Philip press on in spite of his family's lack of cooperation? No, I was just being realistic. I explained to him that he could determine to pursue personal-growth goals regardless of their attitudes; not to do so, I told him, would prove ruinous. Pursuing those personal-growth goals would require that he become a reflective thinker whose game plan superseded his family's frustrating intrusions. Philip needed to be an initiator, not a reactor.

Be an Initiator, Not a Reactor

When I was about thirteen, I attended Bible study classes on Sunday evenings at my church. At the close of each week's lesson my teacher, Mr. Jenkins, would give us an assignment for the next week. I recall one particularly interesting question he asked us to ponder: "Why did Judas choose to betray Christ?"

To find the answer to this question, I did what any other self-respecting thirteen-year-old would do: I asked my dad to tell me what I should say. He could make me look brilliant!

But Dad's response was not what I wanted. Pulling a book off the shelf, Dad turned to a chapter and said, "Read these pages, and in a couple of days let me know what you think."

My thoughts were predictable. *Aw, Dad. Don't make me go through this tomfoolery. You know the answer to the question, so just tell it to me!*

Reading my mind, he said, "If you let someone else do your thinking for you, you'll never really know what you believe. When you learn to reason for yourself, you can be a leader rather than a faceless member of the pack."

Each of us enters the world as a reactor; our earliest years are typified by dependency. We look to parents, siblings, friends, and teachers to direct us in how to feel and think and behave. Even when we do something original, we usually check it out with someone: "Did you see what I just did?" "What do you think about this?" "I hope my parents don't get too mad about this!" Our basic sense of ethics and morality is learned as we register others' ideas about our many choices.

At one point, a trusted authority or friend needs to step forward with the message, "It's time to see what you can do for yourself. Take some initiative." This is accomplished in school as children are taught to be proficient in reading and writing. It is done at home when kids are given greater responsibility in chores and matters of personal hygiene. It is also accomplished when parents and teachers back away long enough to allow children to use their own methods of problem solving.

If we didn't learn to take some initiative as children, we are ill-equipped to face difficult circumstances as adults. We tend to think, *Won't someone solve this problem for me?* When someone doesn't, we are susceptible to anger or fear or worry or guilt.

Philip nodded as we discussed his bitterness. "Without question," I said, "you've lived with a set of circumstances that could create tension in virtually anyone. And very naturally, you've wished for someone to bail you out of those problems. Instead, you're on your own, so you protest about the unfairness of it all."

"Well, it's *not* fair," he said. "For instance, I try *hard* to be a good husband to Joanie, but I just don't feel like she shares my commitment to our marriage. You'd *never* catch me being as critical or whiny as she is. But when I talk with her about changing, she gives me blank stares. I'm real tired of being the one who has to hold the relationship together."

"Then you may have no other option but to be bitter," I said.

"Huh?"

"You're making a good case to justify your bitterness, so go ahead and keep it."

"But that makes no sense. I thought you would tell me how to keep from feeling that way."

Philip wanted me to step forward and solve his problems, but I was not taking his bait. I knew he needed to decide for himself if he would continue entertaining his negative emotions.

Each person needs to seize the freedom to go before God, pondering what the direction of his or her life will be. Have you done this? When you have a history of contemplating such matters, you will react less to the prevailing sentiment.

Young Jesus' relationship with God was so important to Him, He did not want it to be dictated by others. That's why He spent so much time at the temple that Passover Week.

Once the travelers began emptying the city at the end of the holiday, Jesus saw His golden chance. Now He could find the same teachers He had listened to during Passover and speak much more intimately with them. At first He only located one or two and politely asked for their time. He was such a well-kept, likable kid they couldn't say no. But it was only a brief time before they realized He was hardly like any other twelve-year-old. His questions astonished them. He was tagged as a prodigy, and soon several of the religious elite gathered around Him to hear what was on His mind.

The Q-and-A sessions lasted hours. Occasionally someone would bring some food, and the interruption would allow them to laugh and talk about lighter matters. But always Jesus would get back to the more serious subjects. Who knows what He asked! He and the scholars surely discussed the doctrines of sin and atonement and the need for the law. They probably explored the symbolisms of the various feasts and sacrifices, and as the professors explained their concepts they were met with one penetrating question after another.

Undoubtedly, more than one professor was stumped by Jesus' unusual queries, so colleagues were called in to help, and eventually many teachers were enthralled with this young genius from the small northern town. His questions about the Messiah and the writings of the prophets prompted them to talk freely among themselves; in this way Jesus heard the differing thoughts held by the various factions within the ruling religious bodies.

As night fell one would ask if He should be going home yet. He assured them that because of the slow pace of the travelers from Nazareth, He would have no trouble catching up with them, even if they had two or three days' headstart. The men would chuckle and shake their heads, and one would offer Him an extra room for the night.

After three days, when Joseph and Mary realized that Jesus was not part of their enclave, they probably panicked. They hurried back to Jerusalem and began to search for Him until one of them probably said, "I'll bet I know where He is; let's go back to the temple. He's probably there, bending the ear of some poor professor." They may have remembered that He had said He would try to meet with some of the teachers, but they had not taken Him seriously.

Once they arrived at the temple, they might have stood a moment to observe His interaction with the scholars.

Then Mary stepped forward and said, "Son, why have You done this to us?"

The innocence of His response probably caught them

off guard. He said, in effect, "Didn't you realize I want to know all that can be humanly known about My heavenly Father?" Surely they were genuinely amazed that He was this intent on learning things that most twelve-year-olds rarely thought about. Just when they thought they had Him figured out, they realized He was different in ways they could not yet comprehend.

By asking the teachers probing questions, Jesus sifted out their many ideas, clinging to the notions that would allow Him to find God's truth.

Reflective thinkers thrive on challenges to their beliefs.

Accept Challenge As Stimulating

Reflective thinkers know that questions and difficulties can either eliminate weak notions or strengthen good ones. Either way, they come out ahead. We know that Jesus was not one to back down when others challenged His habits or beliefs. He was so confident in His thoughts and abilities that He gladly rose to the task when confronted by a skeptic or cynic. He had spent so much time as a boy formulating His thoughts, He was undaunted in the face of differing perspectives.

Christ's confidence stands in stark contrast to the average person's discomfort with challenges to his or her beliefs. Whereas Jesus saw disruptions as a chance to grow and teach, we tend to see disruptions as threats. We can respond very defensively at that point, using blame or sarcasm or rationalization to ward off the discomfort of having to think deeply about what we believe or why we are making a certain decision.

Philip told me he deeply resented his wife's questioning his decisions.

"No one really likes having his views called into question," I admitted, "but I'm wondering if you can determine that there may be value in knowing her perspective, even if it turns out that she is wrong."

He shook his head slowly. "I'm not sure I could learn to take kindly to her challenges. I just hate having to justify myself to her."

"Ease up on your need to justify, Philip. The worst that could happen is that you might have to admit you were wrong, at which point you could make a needed adjustment. But if you decide to hold firmly to your ways, you could choose to let her be what she is even while you move forward in your personal resolve."

Philip smiled as he responded, "So you're saying I can *choose* to see the value in reflective thinking. Why did I know you'd say something like that!"

By allowing challenges, we demonstrate an awareness that our logic is not always airtight, and even if it is we can acknowledge differing ideas. Such openness implies that we never want to stop learning. We realize we have not yet arrived at perfection, so there is room for new input. As we show others our willingness to contemplate varying points of view, we establish ourselves as fair-minded, and ultimately our leadership and influence increases.

Being open to challenge, though, also means we are willing to risk exposing our ignorance. Once we put ideas or perceptions on the table, we may come to realize that another perspective is more appropriate than our own. We may need to admit our error. Can we do that? It may not be easy. It would require setting aside our need to appear to be "all together." We'll look imperfect.

I recall a particularly obnoxious moment in my own life when I was called on the carpet by one who was wiser than I was. I was in graduate school, and perhaps you are aware that most graduate students believe they know everything. I was in that mode during those days, just as I had been unwilling to admit my weaknesses before that. During a group discussion a fellow student expressed how she was struggling in her personal life as she tried to keep even-tempered while talking to her daughter about dating problems. I chimed in with my brilliance, telling her that she just needed to decide in advance that she knew better than the teenager.

Midway through my speech the professor interrupted. "Mr. Carter, why do you feel it necessary to be so sure of things? Can't you allow someone else the time to process her own doubt?"

I sat there red-faced, realizing how right he was. I had illustrated my need to simplify life by quickly tying down this woman's problem with a quick fix. I had yet to fully appreciate the value of openly struggling for answers to personal issues. In time, I learned that we all need the privilege of wrestling with hard questions. And we all need the desire to know the truth.

A Hunger to Know the Truth

Do you know the truth of God's purpose for your life? Have you contemplated the difference between God's plan for good and Satan's intent for evil? Are you willing to search for answers to hard questions about suffering and rejection? Do you know the deeper doctrines of the faith, the ones related to Christ's return, or the purpose of worship, or the character of God? As you learn these truths, you will be more internally motivated.

I gave Philip an analogy. "Suppose I was about to take you to dinner with a friend of mine, and prior to meeting him, I asked you to refrain from any alcohol consumption in his presence. You might think of me as one of those rule-giving Christians whose favorite word is *don't*. But then I go on to explain that this friend recently lost a son in a car crash involving a drunk driver. At that point your motivation would shift. You would no longer see me as an arbitrary rule-giver but as a kind and sensitive friend. Knowing the reason for my request makes all the difference.

"In the same way," I continued, "God is never arbitrary or finicky in His directives. There is always a purpose to His teachings."

"I've heard Christian teachings all my life, but I've rarely taken the time to concentrate on the truth behind those teachings," Philip admitted. "Maybe that's why I've had such little success in setting aside problems like bitterness."

"Knowing *what* to do is never very motivating until you've come to terms with the reasoning behind it. Before you go any further in your Christian walk it will be important for you to explore the roots of each behavior to determine if it really makes sense."

Philip was able to give up much of his tension after he spent time in prayer and meditation on subjects like forgiveness and servitude and healthy assertiveness. He later told me he was no longer interested in handling Christian teachings like window dressing. He wanted his beliefs to come from the heart.

What behaviors are you attempting to apply *without* the benefit of reflective thinking? Are you attempting to act confidently without really knowing the source of that confidence? Have you been trained to forgive without understanding why forgiveness is a better choice than chronic anger? Do you know what it means to find hope in the knowledge of Christ's soon return?

Be willing to search for the practical application behind the bedrock truths of the Christian faith. Take time to read, to question knowledgeable persons, to withstand others' questioning of you.

Be careful, though. As you search for the meaning behind your behaviors you are likely to encounter false teachings. Some people have concocted strange reasons for pursuing good behavior. It is still good to know what these persons believe, but be sure that their versions of truth are consistent with God's truth as revealed in Scripture.

In any area of thought you will find diverse opinions. Surely young Jesus did not agree completely with the teachers at the temple, yet He remained with them three days. His disagreement with some of their concepts spurred Him to formulate more suitable ideas of His own.

So before dismissing alien ideas, mull them over as you pray that God will guide you toward His ways.

ANTICIPATING OTHERS' REACTIONS

Luke tells us that the Jewish teachers were amazed at the understanding Jesus showed in deep theological and philosophical matters. He concluded his story about Jesus' childhood by saying that Jesus continued growing "in wisdom and stature, and in favor with God and men" (Luke 2:52).

You, too, can find favor as you demonstrate an eagerness to know what is right. Though some of us are intellectually lazy, we can appreciate those who are willing to think for themselves. You will increase your stature and influence with others as you become known as a reflective thinker.

We also know, though, that the religious intellects who were impressed by the twelve-year-old thinker were very threatened by Him twenty years later. His reasoning was so solid that He repeatedly shot holes in their long-standing traditions. Then, instead of praising Him for enlightening them, they became adversaries of the worst sort. Be prepared for rejection as you express your beliefs. But be prepared, too, as you become a reflective thinker, to grow in your spiritual maturity and to discover what is truth.

His Grace:

Jesus and the Accused Woman

John 8:1–11

The young chaplain seemed preoccupied and nervous as he kissed his wife good-bye and tousled his children's hair. He normally did not leave for work after suppertime, but tonight he was going out to be an official witness of a hanging at the prison where he worked, a task he had done only two times before. His wife was somber as she wished him well, and the kids . . . well, they weren't aware of the specifics of Daddy's duty, so they just assumed he had a special meeting that would keep him out until after bedtime.

Once inside the ominous prison complex, the guards escorted the chaplain to the small holding cell where John, a heavyset man over six feet tall, waited. Although no one was in a jovial mood, John smiled as he greeted his guest. Soon the guards brought dinner, and John asked his chaplain friend to join him. At John's request, the menu was fried shrimp and chocolate cake.

The chaplain could barely move the food around on his plate, but John was ravenous, as usual. He ate twenty-three shrimp and two large pieces of cake!

The hanging was set to occur at one minute past midnight, and it was now just a little past eight o'clock, so the chaplain took it upon himself to speak reflectively. "John, we've known this day was coming for quite some time. How are you feeling about it right now?"

A somberness overcame the man as he spoke slowly and softly. "I killed a man. That's a fact I can't change. And now I'm being asked to pay for it with my own life. That's what the justice system requires, so I accept my fate. I wish it hadn't come to this, but I'm ready to die." John's peers had judged him, and he was willing to accept their verdict.

In biblical times, an adulterous woman was in a similar state when she was brought before Jesus. She needed God's grace as desperately as John did.

THE WOMAN WHO RECEIVED GOD'S GRACE

Each time Jesus traveled to Jerusalem He was assured of harassment by the religious elite. On one such visit He approached the temple early in the morning, only to be confronted by a particularly cynical group of Pharisees. "We've got Jesus cornered this time," they laughed to themselves. "We'll put Him in a position of either having to ascribe to the law He seems to disdain or to side with a harlot. Either way He'll have egg on His face!"

Earlier that day, they had accosted a woman known to be sexually vulnerable and coerced her into coming with them to see Jesus. The scene must have been ugly as she cried in protest, shamefully aware that these men considered her a complete low-life. But being grossly outnumbered, she had succumbed to their threats and made her way begrudgingly through the streets leading to the temple.

"There He is! There's Jesus! He claims to be a friend of sinners, but let's see how foolish He'll look once we ask Him if He wants to be friends with this adulterous woman." Clutching the woman by the arms, two Pharisees pushed her toward Jesus, and with a look of disgust one said, "Jesus, this woman has been caught in adultery." He paused to allow everyone to form a vivid picture of what that scene must have looked like, then he went on. "Now, Moses commanded us to stone such women. What do You say?"

Pleased with themselves, the two Pharisees waited smugly for an awkward reply.

But Jesus fooled them. Instead of speaking immediately, He stooped to scribble on the ground. He may have written the names of the men present. He may have written some of the commandments. He was clearly communicating, *Guys, don't think you can burst onto My path and get Me rattled.*

This perturbed the Pharisees. "Well, Jesus, what's Your answer? What do You have to say this time?" They were annoyed that He did not step directly into their neatly laid trap.

Jesus allowed their anxiety to reach fever pitch before answering in a calm voice, "He who is without sin among you, let him throw a stone at her first" (John 8:7). Then He continued writing in the dust.

Bitterness welled up inside the Pharisees: *He's done it again. He's put the monkey onto our backs.* Not daring to look at one another, they each dropped the rocks they had picked up along the way and silently shuffled off. The crowd of onlookers didn't know what to do either. Jesus was not the type who wanted them to jeer at the men or applaud derisively. And besides, that poor woman was still standing before Jesus. He had said nothing to her yet. What would He do next?

The woman was dirty; her clothes were rumpled because of the men's rough handling. Hair tumbled over her face as her head hung morosely.

Jesus walked toward her. He knew she had lived down to the low expectations others had for her, yet He reckoned that she was a valuable person who could be a wonderful witness to His grace and forgiveness. Compassion overwhelmed Him as He gently touched her shoulder.

She didn't know what to expect. Would He lecture her about her sinfulness? Women in that day were not highly regarded anyway, and a woman of her reputation stood no chance of being treated with dignity. She probably thought, *Go ahead, Jesus. Tell me what I need to hear. I'm a nobody who deserves nothing but scorn. Ask around. Anyone who knows me will tell You that. I'm a loser. I've got it coming.* Her tears were so plentiful she could barely make out Jesus' facial features.

As Jesus began to speak, she was struck by the kindness in His voice. "Woman, where are those accusers of yours? Has no one condemned you?" (John 8:10).

What a strange question. But wait, He's making a point. Those men were so eager to leave, they said nothing more about her. Cautiously shaking her head, she spoke quietly, "No one, Lord."

Jesus gave a gentle smile. "Neither do I condemn you; go and sin no more" (John 8:11).

His words caught her completely off guard. *That's it? No lecture? No scolding?* As she walked slowly toward her home the woman must have been bewildered. *What just happened to me? In the span of just a few minutes I've gone from feeling lower than low to feeling a strange comfort. I'm not sure what Jesus is about, but I've got to know Him personally. Thank You, God, thank You.* Tears of thankfulness and hope streamed down her face.

This incident captures my mind and heart in ways few

others do. It reminds me that Jesus is quite unlike anyone I would ever encounter. He is the standard-bearer for grace, God's unmerited favor.

I like to think I would respond just as Jesus did, but I know myself well enough to admit that forgiveness is not always my initial reaction to wrongdoing. Several years ago it became apparent that a family friend was not going to repay a personal loan I had made to him. I'm not wealthy, and I'm certainly not in the banking business, but I had trusted him to keep his end of our agreement. Yet after that loan he began avoiding me. Not only did I lose the money, but our relationship was broken as well. I knew forgiveness was the route I needed to take, but I didn't want to do it. Forgiveness seemed too good for him. After all, he'd cheated me.

Have you ever been disappointed by someone and all efforts to remedy the problem have failed? Can you be forgiving? Can you live with the loose ends? Jesus had the satisfaction of knowing that the adulterous woman appreciated what He could offer her. Would He have been forgiving if she had not been so receptive? I believe so. Even knowing this, I still hesitate to forgive when it just doesn't seem fair.

I recently counseled a woman, Paula, in her mid-thirties, who was looked up to by other women because she could be counted on to organize Bible studies and other ministry activities at her church. Friendly and outgoing, she could converse freely with virtually anyone. She sought counseling only because her older sister, Katy, insisted that she come.

I began by asking her to tell me about the relationship between Katy and herself. Instead she immediately told me, "Katy and her husband separated over two years ago, and no one seems to know how to handle her situation. They're divorced now, but I've been against it from day one.

"It's not that I can't handle the fact that she's now a single mom; I can deal with that. But Katy has such a temper; I feel she set herself up for this fall. She can get mad at anyone, including me, over the most minor problems! I've put up with her attitude all my life, and I'm growing increasingly resentful whenever I'm around her."

"I assume you've communicated your thoughts to your sister and it didn't go over too well?"

"Oh, yes!" Paula replied. "But the more we talk, the less we get along. She knows how I feel about her bad temper, but she just doesn't make the effort to mend broken fences."

Making an educated guess I said, "And she tells you that she doesn't want your input because she's heard it all before. Is that why there is a rift between the two of you?"

"That's it. On one hand, I agree that I have to accept her because, after all, she *is* my sister. But, Dr. Carter, I've got my Christian principles to stand on. How am I going to teach good morals to my own children if they don't see me holding firmly to solid beliefs? Katy's got to understand that we just can't condone wishy-washy commitments."

Before you are too hard in your reaction to Paula's feelings toward her sister, remind yourself that it is easy to talk about the merits of forgiveness until you have regular, ongoing interactions with someone who walks a different path from yours. You may have a relative whose drinking problem will not go away. You may know about the promiscuous behavior of a niece or nephew. Perhaps your spouse has shown many weaknesses or imperfections that annoy you.

When you come face to face with such persons, can you think in terms of forgiveness?

I wish I knew what crossed Jesus' mind when the adulteress was introduced to Him. His views about marriage and lust and purity of thought were very well known. Jesus was a man of strong conviction. Yet, in spite of the fact that this woman stood for the opposite of everything He taught, He openly expressed tenderness and forgiveness to her. How unpredictable Jesus must have been to those who thought they had Him figured out! That's the way I want to be. I want to practice His grace, and to do so I must learn to forgive.

LEARNING TO FORGIVE

Grace and forgiveness are unnatural to most people because we have been trained early in life to build our reputations and self-esteem around performances. "If I can do the right activities and create the desired impressions," the reasoning goes, "I will prove myself worthy of acceptance." Paula had believed this all her life.

"When I was a kid," she explained, "I always felt Katy and I were on different wavelengths. She was the kind of person who constantly pushed her limits. She knew what would make our parents mad, and she would do wrong sometimes for the sheer thrill of seeing them react. It drove the family nuts!"

"She gave you lots of reasons to be bitter?"

"She really did," Paula explained. "I always found it hard to like her. I wasn't perfect, but I realized that the best way to get along was to do what was right. Whereas Katy was erratic in her schoolwork, I was conscientious. My parents could count on me. I was prompt, and I was courteous to adults."

Can you relate to Paula's upbringing? Or were you a Katy? People who struggle with forgiveness tend to be more like Paula—they believe rules are made to be followed and performance is the way to prove you are good.

Don't get me wrong. I respect people who respect authority. Structure, morals, and discipline are all part of a successful life. Yet if we place such a powerful emphasis on correct performances and lose relational harmony, we can have too much of a good thing.

To become more forgiving, we need to recognize our own need for grace and forgiveness.

Our Need for Grace and Forgiveness

John's execution occurred in 1958. Several years earlier John had stood in the state courtroom before a judge, knowing he was guilty but not knowing if the judge would give him a life sentence or death. When he heard the words, "You shall be hanged by the neck until you are dead," John's mind became a blur. He had always had a temper, and he had told himself that one day he'd better calm down, but he had never dreamed his problems would drive him to the extreme. He was very despondent and angry at himself for falling to such low depths.

Upon entering prison, John was confined to death row and eventually became acclimated to the other prisoners and the routine of life under strict security. He and his lawyer went through the usual process of filing legal appeals, but as time wore on John realized he was a marked man who needed to ready himself for the inevitable.

Once the young chaplain was assigned to this prison, he made almost daily visits to death row, and he focused on John. Realizing John was not a Christian the chaplain nonetheless sensed a willingness in him to know a little something about his Creator. The two began studying the Bible together, and during the following months John began to understand the basic teachings of Scripture. Numerous times they discussed the plan of salvation, and finally one summer day John declared, "I'm ready. I want to accept Jesus as my personal Savior. I know it won't change the sentence I've been given, but I want to be saved."

John and the chaplain knelt on the concrete floor of that death row cell, and John asked Jesus to come into his heart; his prayer indicated a genuine understanding of his sin and his need for the Savior. A huge smile crossed his face as he stood again, and from that point on John was a different person. He had experienced God's overwhelming grace.

God's grace originates from His desire to illustrate that His love is so great, it can be shown no matter what sin is involved. His grace is an extension of His merciful nature. But humans are not God. When we show forgiveness, it is not because we can align ourselves to God's perfect, merciful character. Rather, we extend forgiveness to others because we feel so appreciative to be recipients of God's grace, we want others to feel the same way. While we were still sinners, God sent His Son to die for us. Any kindness that does not flow from this understanding is pushed along by manipulative motives.

If a man assumes that his business ethics are virtually perfect yet he decides to forgive a partner who has cheated him, his reaction is honorable yet it could easily cause him to feel a puffed-up pride: *I hope this person realizes how good I have been to him.* But when this same man recognizes that he, too, has flirted with corner-cutting temptations, he identifies with his partner's need and he becomes a fellow learner rather than a manipulator.

Can you align yourself vicariously with persons in need of grace, knowing that you, too, could struggle similarly? Consider these examples:

- You may never have been in a major depression, but you have a family member struggling with this problem. Rather than giving the relative a "What's wrong with you?" talk, you can gently encourage him or her as you admit to yourself that you are fully capable of the same struggle if the right circumstances come along.

- Your spouse tells you he or she has lied to you about money matters. You feel very frustrated because you have never lied about money. Yet perhaps you can admit times when you have tried to project a false image of yourself in other matters.

Grace is made possible only as you genuinely identify with the one receiving it. This may create a question in your mind: *Are you suggesting that Jesus identified personally with the adulterous woman's misdeeds?* No, but Jesus did identify with her need for affection, affirmation, and approval. Her means of fulfilling these needs was poor, but rather than honing in on her poor coping skills, He identified with her need for love.

As Paula and I discussed this concept, she became painfully honest with me. "You know how competitive sisters can be. When we were growing up, especially in our teen and early adult years, I made a deliberate decision not to be like Katy. I didn't want to identify in any way with her because I could see that she was headed down the wrong paths."

"In a very real way this attitude helped you because you don't have the same track record of poor choices," I reflected. "But maybe you've gone too far in removing yourself from her. Your detachment can lead you dangerously close to a better-than-thou attitude."

Paula sat quietly for a moment, then admitted, "I don't want to project that kind of attitude. But it's hard for me to think of myself as being just like Katy, especially since I've made such a deliberate choice to be different."

"In lifestyle matters you are not like her," I replied, "yet you have the same need for approval and self-expression, though she pursues these needs differently from you." I went on to explain that Katy's temper was driven by a craving to be respected or to be taken seriously.

My discussion with Paula was a reflection of my own understanding about myself and about human nature in general. You may be like me in the sense that it is hard to admit just how wrong your thoughts can be. I don't want to be known as a person who lives with negatives, yet honesty requires me to admit that, given the right circumstances, I could be just as awful as the next person. I have put safeguards on myself and created ways to maintain proper accountability, and that keeps me in line. But can I claim moral superiority over anyone? No. I need God's grace just as desperately as everyone else. Whatever success I have had, whatever failures I have avoided, cannot erase the fact that I am just as capable of sin as the next person. We are all in the same boat.

Each individual is unique in behaviors and choices, yet at the inner core we are all the same. As we identify with each other's human needs we can communicate: *Though different, we are equal.*

We all have to watch the tendency to make performance more important than relationships. Instead, the opposite should be true.

Relationships Have Priority over Performance

Above all else, Christianity is about relationships. God has no need for any input from you or me, yet He invites us to share life with Him for no reason other than the fact that He wants to do so. When we meet Him face to face in heaven, our bliss will be anchored in the thrill of merely being in His presence, offering worship. Yet people who have difficulty forgiving are usually more interested in performances than relationships.

Is it wrong to have strong performance goals for yourself and those close to you? Absolutely not. Scripture is full of instruction regarding the ways to manage morality, work, and talents. It offers solid advice on performances within the home, in a church, within friendships. God knows that without His guidance, we will easily turn toward poor choices, so He is very implicit.

But is performance the sum total of Scripture's emphasis? If you listened exclusively to legalistically minded persons you might assume this to be the case. From the beginning of humankind's existence, God has openly spelled out His rules for right and wrong. In His first sentence to Adam, He explained that Adam was not to eat of the Tree of Knowledge of Good and Evil. By this He communicated that He was the one who declared what correct living is and that Adam was obliged to recognize that he could not take that role upon himself. When Adam sinned, God instituted a system of consequences to underscore His displeasure with disobedience. This shows that He wants us to live with good performances.

But understand one major fact: Adam was not supposed to be alive after defying God! He had brought the death sentence upon himself.

If God's primary focus was good performances, you

and I would not exist. We conform so poorly to God's perfect standards we deserve only to be removed from Him. But God's chief aim is relationships; He so desires to live in love with you and me He sets aside His own standards. He does not cease to believe in the correctness of those standards because His mind does not change. Yet, He goes so far as to accept substitutionary death so we can maintain life with Him. The first act of substitutionary death was performed in Eden when God killed an animal to make coverings for Adam and Eve. The last act was when He did the unthinkable and offered His Son on our behalf.

Performance *is* important to God, but relationships are His ultimate goal.

I explained to Paula, "Katy has made many choices that run counter to godly standards. Does God like divorce? No. Does He delight in rebellion? No. Does He enjoy her wild temper? No. Your sister has certainly fallen short of His standards. Sometimes she does this with full awareness of what it means; sometimes she falls into it unwittingly.

"But who am I to reject her because of her poor choices?" I continued. "As I survey my own life, I see many times when I have fallen short. When I suggest that you forgive your sister I am not asking you to let go of your solid standards. Rather, I am suggesting that you show your sister that you place a higher premium on God's love than her performance. When you do this, you will be imitating the very attitude God takes toward you."

"I run the risk of appearing to condone her choices if I am kind and supportive toward her," she reflected.

I nodded my head to indicate that she was correct in this assessment. She continued, "I've got to decide if it's important to take that risk even if it gives the impression that I'm softening my positions."

"It wouldn't be called forgiveness if her performances conformed to your standards. Show her acceptance in a way that illustrates that you deeply cherish the relationship itself. Undoubtedly there will be times in your own life when you will need the same treatment yourself."

Who in your life needs to know of your priorities? For me it's my wife and children. They need my love and acceptance far more than my correction.

Concentrate on Edification

I know some people who have a tough-as-nails reputation—and they actually like it! They enjoy being known as someone who prefers the pit-bull approach. They are proud to be perfectionistic and demanding. You probably know a few of these folks yourself!

Imagine if Jesus had used tough language right out of the chute with the adulterous woman. "Lady, you should have known you had it coming. When you make the choices you've made, you're going to get burned. Now go clean up your act and get back to Me in a month with an update on how you're doing." He would have been justified in His words, but He would never have seen the woman again.

People need encouragement. We are motivated more

by compliments than complaints. We need affirmation, a word that says, "I'm still with you."

This need has its roots in our dependency, a personality trait common to each person. Consider the birthday of an infant. As the child is born, what do the adults instinctively do? They care for the child, scurrying to do whatever it takes to make him or her feel comfortable. They feed the child, bathe the child, hold the child, caress the child. They make eye contact constantly and speak endearing words. The child is totally dependent and must have this treatment in order to survive and thrive.

What would you think about the person who treats a newborn baby differently? Suppose the infant is just laid in a crib and left alone in a far room except for feeding time. Once fed, the baby is put back in the empty room. You'd cry abuse! No child deserves such treatment, and no adult could in good conscience believe that a child could manage with bland, functional care.

Are adults any different from that infant? In some ways yes. We are not as helpless. Yet even adults have ongoing dependencies. We need that same acceptance and affirmation and encouragement. The required dosage is different, but we still have that inborn need to feel connected.

This realization caused Paula to rethink her approach toward Katy. I explained, "You need to ask yourself: 'What do I want Katy to sense in me?' You want her to respect the lifestyle you stand for, but she will never do so until she knows you are on her team."

"I know you're right. As I've heard you explain your ideas, I've realized that I don't want to be known as a judge or a critic. I want my sister to feel she can lean on me." But then, cocking her head to one side, Paula asked, "How do I change my intentions when I've spent years fighting with her?"

"Let Katy know you've done a lot of thinking about your past reactions, and you are determined to be more forgiving. You will only give advice if asked, and you will refrain from judging her when she clearly contradicts your beliefs. This should certainly get her attention."

"I'll say it would. It would be good for her to hear me say it because she would be less cautious with me, and it would be good for me as well since I'd become more openly committed to following through on my intentions."

You will find no end to the numbers of people in need of grace. And you will probably realize that Christianity "in the trenches" is less consumed with correctness than it is with the many intangibles of the faith . . . patience, forgiveness, tolerance, kindness, goodness, and the like.

Others will be blessed as you demonstrate this characteristic so perfectly modeled by Christ. But be prepared. You won't be the same as your commitment to grace deepens.

On the night before he was executed, John reminded the chaplain of the day he had first trusted Jesus, and they talked about the feelings of regret he had for his past misdeeds. Then they discussed the relief he felt, knowing that Jesus would be waiting for him in just a few moments to escort him as His own before the Father.

About fifteen minutes before midnight the guard indicated the time had come for John to take his final steps down the hall. But before leaving, John and the chaplain sang, "What a Friend We Have in Jesus" and "Amazing Grace," two of John's favorite hymns.

John prayed a final prayer, brief and simple: "Dear God, in just a few minutes I am coming to be with You forever. Thank You that Jesus is my Savior. Please bless the family of the man I wronged, and God, please bless my mama and my sister. Take good care of them all. And Lord, help the people who are about to hang me not to feel bad about what they have to do. Amen."

Within minutes John walked into the execution chamber, and the deed was done.

That young chaplain was Ed Carter, my dad. At the time he had shielded me from knowing what he was doing at that late-night meeting. But years later, when I was a college student, he talked with me about his experiences with people like John.

I was an idealist who struggled with the idea of capital punishment. "Dad, how were you able to handle your emotions when you had to witness the death of someone like John? Didn't it just eat you up inside?"

"I can tell you that an experience like that is one you can never feel comfortable with," he said. "But I saw myself as being in a unique position. God used me to show His grace at a time when it was desperately needed. I was God's representative at that moment, and I took my role very seriously. That thought alone kept me from being distracted by any outside controversies or by any of my emotions."

Dad's statement stuck in my mind: *I was God's repre-sentative.*

John had been woefully lacking for friends who thought of themselves as representing God. To the contrary, his early years had been dominated by a bitter, abusive rela-tionship with his father. The town thugs had taken him in, and John had assumed that the only way to be somebody was to be the meanest of the bunch. He had lived out his pitiable life's script to the max, becoming an angry, hostile man who proved how despicable he could be by taking another man's life.

How fortunate John was that a young chaplain saw himself as being God's representative whose role was to be a deliverer of grace. How fortunate I am that I have known people who also took that same task upon them-selves for me.

I cannot think of a clearer way to describe the driving force behind Jesus' personality. Whether He was standing before the woman caught in adultery or waiting at heaven's gate to greet John or whether He is attending to the daily concerns of Les Carter, He knows His mission: "I am God's chosen representative. Let Me show you who the Father is."

Like my dad, I am a Christian, one who seeks after the heart of Christ. And my prayer is the same as his: "Thank You, God, that You would allow me to be aligned to Jesus. May I be His worthy representative."

— Appendix —

Discussion Questions

Use the following discussion questions to help you focus more intently in your own individual study of the character of Christ. Or use the questions as a guide for group study sessions.

Chapter 2
His Humility
(Read Revelation 5:1–14; Revelation 21; and Luke 2:1–20.)

1. The angels who sang before the shepherds on the Bethlehem hillside had been privileged to sing to God in heaven. They knew fully who Jesus was and why He had entered humanity. What thoughts prompted them to be so enthusiastic in their praise?

2. Why did Christ find humility to be such a necessary ingredient in His personality?

3. Pride and self-preoccupied thinking can be manifested in a broad array of behaviors and personality traits. List several of the ways pride can show itself in your life.

4. Since humility is the opposite of pride, consider

again your responses to the previous question, then list the opposites of those prideful traits. Can you see how humility is at the base of each one?

5. Humility is often thought of as servitude, yet it is much more than that. Suppose, for instance, that you have been rejected by someone whose love you desire. How could humility help you manage your emotions at a time like that?

6. Some people have understood humility to mean that you should accept another's foul treatment without complaint. What do you think?

7. How can your commitment to humility positively impact your management of anger?

8. Think of two typical occurrences that might warrant a better response of humility from you. (For instance, "When my husband acts stubbornly, I can respond with just as much stubbornness," or "I'm prone to speaking too abruptly when correcting my kids.")

9. How would your commitment to humility affect your relationship with God, particularly as you worship Him and study His Word?

Chapter 3
His Self-Restraint
(Read Matthew 4:1–11.)

1. Jesus, being fully human, came under Satan's temptation just as you and I do. Do you think He was surprised that Satan had the nerve to tempt Him as he did? Why or why not?

2. It is a fact that we, too, will undergo temptations. How can the simple acknowledgment of this reality help us in our responses to those temptations?

3. Many people refuse to admit the extent of their struggles against their own self-wills. (For instance, we do not like to admit self-centeredness, control, greed, etc.) Why is this?

4. What is the difference between self-restraint and unhealthy suppression of emotions?

5. Consider the following list of common problems. Which ones apply to you?

- Impatience, particularly when your mind is already focused on another project

- Lust, or the craving to be loved and nurtured by someone other than your mate

- Envy or frustration because others have attained what you want

- The need for public approval or acceptance

- A demanding nature

- Criticism and the need to be correct

- Drivenness and the need to complete a task before you can feel satisfied

- Intellectualizing and having to impress others with your knowledge

- Worry and being so anxious that you are too easily displeased

6. Looking back over the items you identified with,

how would your life improve if you could incorporate more self-restraint into your life?

7. Suppose you are talking with someone who complains, "My whole life has consisted of denying myself to the extent that I'm tired of being restrained." How would you counsel this person?

8. Can you think of an example when self-restraint could be set aside in order to allow exploration of new or unusual options?

9. Galatians 2:20 and Philippians 4:11 are two key verses that illustrate the mind-set of self-restraint. What message do you gain from these passages?

Chapter 4
His Kindness
(Read Mark 10:13–16.)

1. Jesus must have been tired at the end of a busy day of teaching, yet He wanted to spend time with the children. Why was this so?

2. Sometimes people can appear to be kind or encouraging when in fact it is just an act or a technique. How can you know when warmth is the real thing?

3. Kindness can be demonstrated by a soft touch or an engaging smile. Can you think of four other ways kindness can be expressed?

4. To communicate kindness, you have to honestly want close ties to others. What inner barriers might keep a person from showing kindness? (For instance, hidden anger or insecurities.)

5. Look at the following illustrations of kindness and consider how you might make some personal adjustments so kindness can be more integral to your relating style.

- You'll touch a friend's shoulder as you engage in pleasant conversation.
- As a person discusses a problem, you'll not be over-eager to tell him or her what to do.
- You will remember simple tidbits of information about a person and later you will ask or comment about them.
- Others, particularly those closest to you, would describe you as an encourager, not a critic.
- Laughter comes easily.
- You are willing to be open in exposing your own tender or sensitive feelings.
- Projects do not have higher priority than relationships.
- You are not uncomfortable when someone expresses his or her need or grief.

6. What might you have to give up to practice more consistent kindness? (For instance, perfectionistic tendencies or a need to achieve.)

7. How can you be kind toward a person who does not seem to want to connect with you?

8. In the days and weeks ahead, what can you do differently as you determine to incorporate a more inviting manner into your relating style?

Chapter 5
His Confidence

(Read John 18:28–38.)

1. During His questioning by Pilate, Jesus showed remarkable confidence. He would not be intimidated in any way. Yet just a few hours earlier when praying at Gethsemane, He had been in great agony. To what can we attribute this change in mood?

2. Pilate attempted to appear confident, yet his haughtiness revealed an uncertainty within. What is the difference between confidence and haughtiness (or arrogance)?

3. What hindrances can keep you from being confident? (For instance, "I worry too much about keeping people happy.")

4. Sometimes you may look confident on the outside, yet you can struggle inwardly with uncertainty. Is this normal? Why or why not?

5. Consider the following indicators of confidence and pick two that you would like to improve upon in your life. How would you be different as you make your adjustments?

- Not quick to justify beliefs when under attack
- Willing to hear others' opinions, even if they are wrong
- Willing to admit wrongs readily
- Willing to speak about personal matters, showing vulnerability

- Being relaxed in a group, even if you do not know everyone there
- Speaking your opinions firmly but without salesmanship or undue persuasion
- Refraining from repeating yourself unnecessarily when making a point
- Not prone to suspicion or distrust

6. The Christian's confidence is not anchored in personal achievement or acclaim, but in his or her righteous standing before God. Why isn't this easy to maintain?

7. Think of someone who does not think as confidently toward you as you would like. How can you remain secure in spite of that person's feelings? How would that security be shown in your behavior?

8. One way to remain confident is to remember that your judges are showing insecurity by virtue of their judgments against you. How can you know that you are not being critical or condescending as you consider this fact?

Chapter 6
His Objectivity
(Read John 4:3–42.)

1. The woman at the well clearly had a troubled past and a scarred reputation. What thoughts do you tend to nurse inwardly when you meet people who are prone to emotional ups and downs?

2. Jesus seemed calm as He related with this woman,

even though she openly violated some of the beliefs He held fervently. How could He do this?

3. Many would argue that if you don't speak up for your own deep convictions, you are quietly condoning the sinfulness of that person's lifestyle. Yet Jesus passed over the opportunity to do this. Why?

4. When someone else is illogical or emotionally charged, it is easy to respond with your own strongly charged emotions. When are you most vulnerable for this to happen?

5. If you were determined to be less emotional in your reaction to others' emotional displays, what positive contributions would you make to your relationship?

6. Picture in your mind the following scenarios. As you consider each one, decide how you can know if you are responding with objectivity.

- A child defiantly says no when you give a clear directive.

- Your spouse is clearly not willing to receive your commonsense feedback.

- No matter how well you explain yourself, your brother-in-law cannot comprehend what you are saying.

7. Think of three common recurring problems that could be managed better as you learn to be more objective in your communications. (For instance, "When my spouse speaks critically of me, I can choose not to respond in kind,

realizing instead that he or she is just in an insecure mood.")

8. Your tone of voice is crucial in showing objectivity. What are some differences between a person's voice tone when he or she is emotionally charged compared with when the person is being objective?

Chapter 7
His Empathy
(Read John 11:1–36.)

1. Jesus became engrossed in Mary's emotions. What did He sense in her that moved Him so deeply?

2. Martha was surely a witness to this scene. The Bible depicts her as an organizer and one more interested in performing tasks. What thoughts do you suppose went through her mind as Jesus wept with Mary?

3. John 11:36 describes the onlookers as saying, "See how He loved him!" They believed Jesus was weeping over Lazarus's death. What do you think? Did the crowd read Jesus accurately? Explain.

4. Notice some key indicators of empathy in the following statements. Which ones do you need to improve on the most?

- You let emotions run their course.
- You do not need to give answers immediately when a person shares matters of a personal nature.
- You are willing to set aside your own agenda in order to tend to another's expressions.

- Achievements receive less attention than emotions and perceptions.
- You are willing to become personally involved with others.
- You will openly communicate your understanding with others.
- Patience is a high priority because you realize it takes time to explore and understand one another's feelings.
- You will read the "behind-the-scenes" meaning of a person's expressions or behaviors.

5. Why is empathy sometimes unnatural?

6. Can you think of four circumstances that occurred recently in your life that could have been opportunities to practice empathy?

7. Who do you know that probably needs a friend like you who is willing to take the time to develop an understanding rapport?

8. Think of a time when you have been successful in showing understanding to a friend or a family member. How did the person act toward you afterward?

9. What will have to be re-prioritized in your life as you commit to being more empathetic?

Chapter 8
His Assertiveness
(Read Mark 11:15–18; Luke 18:18–25; and Luke 19:45–48.)

1. Rarely did Jesus communicate anger with the force

He used that day in the temple. Why did He consider it necessary to speak so strongly then?

2. Read the following examples of assertiveness and consider which ones are more natural for you and which are most difficult:

- You can stand unwaveringly on your convictions.
- When you set boundaries (with children, your mate, a friend), you can do so without excessively justifying your case.
- You can let others know how to specifically meet your needs.
- You can say no and stick to it when you are already overloaded.
- You will do what is right for yourself, even in the face of outside pressure.
- When distractions could easily disrupt your day, you can stick with your plans as you realize the need to remain organized.
- As you express your preferences, you can do so without salesmanship.

3. What part of your life would improve most if you could come to terms with assertiveness?

4. The rich young ruler apparently experienced an abrupt change in emotion (from eagerness to sadness) during his discussion with Jesus (see Matt. 19:16–30). What emotions do you suppose Jesus felt toward him?

5. When Jesus did not plead with the man to reconsider his decision, it could have been interpreted by onlookers

as a lack of concern. How does noncoercive but assertive communication differ from apathy?

6. People with strong convictions often become persuasive as they speak their minds. How can you know when such persuasion is unhealthy?

7. Suppose you are on a tight schedule and your family members seem unconcerned about your time needs. How might you handle the situation assertively? What would be the likely response of your family members?

8. As you become assertive without being coercive, you run the risk that others (spouse, children, friends) may take your feelings less seriously. How can you prevent that from happening without resorting to unhealthy communication practices?

Chapter 9
His Respect
(Read Luke 19:1–10.)

1. Zacchaeus was a difficult man to respect because of his history of making money by gouging fellow countrymen. What traits do you find in people that make it difficult to give them respect?

2. Jesus was able to "read between the lines" and determine that Zacchaeus hungered for someone to love and respect him. What signals could you look for in people you know that would indicate the same thing?

3. Why do we tend to make our respect for others conditional?

4. Consider the many distasteful qualities you may see

in others (for instance, rebellion, passiveness, an argumentative nature, whining, insensitivity). Is it possible to be respectful in the midst of these traits? Why or why not?

5. Suppose a family member is speaking harshly to you and you feel defensive at that moment. How could your commitment to be respectful guide your response?

6. Answer true or false to each of the following statements. Then look at the statements again and consider what you could change in yourself so you could be more consistently respectful.

_____ When people question the validity of my feelings, I can still remain respectful even though I don't like their reactions to me.

_____ I can accept the fact that others' feelings and emotions will not always match mine.

_____ I struggle more than I want with a critical disposition.

_____ Being firm can often bring out harshness in me.

_____ Life has to be fair before I can be cooperative or agreeable.

_____ Once someone acts rejectingly, I can lose my good intentions and respond with either irritability or rejection of my own.

_____ I can clearly detach my emotions when it becomes clear that another person is being irrational with me.

7. How can you know you are not just being phony or suppressing anger when you show respect?

8. Think of someone you know who most needs the gift of respect. How, in the weeks ahead, will you offer respect to that person?

Chapter 10
His Reflective Thinking
(Read Luke 2:40–52.)

1. This passage gives us a unique insight into the human dimension of young Jesus. What caused Him to have such a compelling curiosity that He would stay behind three days to study Scripture with the teachers?

2. Jesus had many questions about the law and the prophets. In other words, He wanted to grasp God's plan for redemption within the context of the big picture. Why is it so important to see the whole picture before analyzing its many separate parts?

3. Many people today practice what I call "passive Christianity." That is, they want others to feed them and keep them motivated to maintain their enthusiasm for godliness. Why is this dangerous?

4. Some find their faith unraveling when they encounter difficult circumstances. Why does this happen? Is this always wrong or bad?

5. Answer true or false to the following statements. Then look back over the statements you've identified as false and consider what goals you could give yourself as you seek to apply wise insights to your life.

_____ When difficulties arise, I can curb my natural inclination to question God's guidance.

_____ I know a lot about the Bible to the extent that it is a true source of comfort when life seems unfair.

_____ I am learning to keep my emotions in check long enough so I can make sense of my frustrations before they get me down.

_____ My understanding of God's plan for my life causes me to live with a patient spirit.

_____ Even though I may not like challenges to my faith, I trust that I can handle them when they do come.

_____ I have developed a well-conceived philosophy of worshiping God.

_____ I don't mind being challenged to explain why I believe as I do.

_____ My spiritual life would certainly improve if I spent less time complaining and more time in quiet contemplation of God.

6. Christianity addresses many matters pertaining to relationships and emotions, yet many Christians struggle in this area. Why does this happen?

7. One way to claim greater ownership of your guiding philosophies is to openly speak of your ideas with those who share life with you. Why is this helpful?

8. Summarize your core thoughts regarding the ways you would like Christianity to influence you in your closest relationships.

Chapter 11
His Grace

(Read John 8:1–11.)

1. While the Pharisees wanted to debate with Jesus about the merits of the law, Jesus wanted nothing to do with that. Why?

2. By showing grace, Jesus ran the risk of being branded liberal or loosely principled. Why was He willing to take that risk?

3. Many Christians today easily endorse the notion of grace, claiming that it is a wonderful gift from God. Yet, when we become aware of another's sinfulness or weakness we can just as easily become rejecting or judgmental. Why is this?

4. Consider the following scenarios and identify the two you would find most difficult to respond to with grace.

- Your children have made poor choices that have brought problems upon them.

- Your mate does not consistently live up to your early expectations.

- While you make the effort to stay in contact with friends, that effort is not reciprocated.

- For years a relative has tarnished family gatherings with a pessimistic approach to life.

- At work you feel you're the only one willing to go the extra mile.

- A good friend wasn't there for you when you were in need.
- You've talked with an acquaintance about some very personal feelings, but now it seems your thoughts are being ignored.

5. For most people, it is easier to receive grace than to give it. Why?

6. What personality traits are most closely associated with grace?

7. Who do you have difficulty in extending grace toward? How would you be different if you committed yourself to practicing this trait?

8. Why do you need grace?